Contents

W9-AVN-892

© Macmillan/McGraw-Hill

What is a Running Record?

"Running Records offer a window into the brains of young readers as their reading skills grow and change. They are one of the most important instruments we could have in our assessment toolbox." (Connie Hebert)

Taking a Running Record is a method which closely observes and evaluates a student's oral reading. Running Records help teachers identify a student's reading level, style, and strategy use. They help determine a student's independent (easy), instructional, and frustrational (hard) reading levels and provide information on how the student is processing the text. Using the cueing system and classifying errors as *meaning, structure,* or *visual,* you can discern patterns of effective and ineffective strategy use. You can also obtain a reading accuracy percentage, error rate, and a self-correction rate from this assessment. Running Records provide the necessary data for teachers to plan appropriate instruction to meet individual needs.

It is important to establish a permanent assessment area in your classroom. Arranging an assessment table with the appropriate resources will enable you to check a student's progress at a moment's notice. When materials are out and accessible, they are used more often. Be sure to have your Running Record passages copied and your Benchmark Books ready to use. Keep your Conversion Table and recording forms available as well.

How often should teachers take Running Records?

Children's reading levels change quickly, so running record data is only valid for a period of four weeks. Running Records should be taken every three to four weeks to monitor progress and document the student's developing strategies. Set aside time to take one Running Record per day so that this becomes an ongoing assessment.

Using the Running Record Form

The form on page 10 allows you to compile information and analyze the results of the Running Record. It also allows you to note the strategies used when encountering unknown words and making an error.

© Macmillan/McGraw-Hill

What are the procedures for taking a Running Record?

1. Read along in your copy of the text as the student reads aloud.

2. Record the student's name, age, and the date on the recording sheets.

3. Introduce the Benchmark Book by reading the title and discussing the cover.

4. Do not expand upon the content during this introduction.

5. Read the short introduction provided on the first page of each Benchmark Book or before each passage.

6. Before the student reads, say this prompt:

    I would like you to read to me. Read the words aloud. If you come to a word you don't know, do whatever you would normally do to figure it out if you were alone. While you read, I am going to take notes about the good things you are doing. When you are finished reading I will ask you to tell me about what you have read, answer questions, or fill out a graphic organizer.

7. Without verbal comment, mark a check for each word read accurately and note any substitutions, omissions, additions, and self-corrections using the conventions that are in the marking key code on **page 8.**

8. Do not prompt the student in any way. Any student response should be recorded on the sheet. If you need to say the word for the student, then score it as an error, or you can advise your student to try the word again.

9. Mark the errors with the coding conventions shown below and tally them in the error column. Classify each error in the **MSV** column and mark it as **M, S,** or **V.**

10. When the student stops reading, quickly total the number of miscues and self-corrections, and then calculate the reading accuracy percentage and self-correction rate.

11. If the student shows an in-depth understanding of the text, with a retell score of 4 and a 95% accuracy rate, take another Running Record at the next level higher. If the student achieves the same results, you know the text is at his/her independent level and not appropriate for reading instruction. Continue moving up a level until an instructional and frustrational level have been established. If you have been able to establish an instructional level, you must continue testing your student until his/her frustrational level has been identified. Stop testing once you are able to ascertain your student's highest instructional level. The goal is to obtain an authentic instructional reading level and an independent and frustrational level as well.

12. Use the recording sheets provided in this book. The leveled text appears on the running record form to simplify the recording of miscues.

© Macmillan/McGraw-Hill

What Are the Cueing Systems That Students Use to Read Text?

There are three cueing systems that students need to use in order to be successful readers.

- **Meaning (M):** *Does it make sense?* The student uses the meaning or the general context of the story/sentence as cues.
- **Structure (S):** *Does it sound right?* The structure of the text (up to and including the error) should be an acceptable English language construction.
- **Visual (V):** *Does it look right* (match the print)? Visual cues in the text are the visual appearances of the letters and the words.

Meaning Cues

The meaning and general context of the story are used as cues.

Ask: Does the error make sense in the context of the story?

Text	Errors		Cues Used	
✓ ✓ ✓ ✓ tigers ✓ ✓ ✓ I like to see lions at the zoo.	E	SC	E	SC
	1		MS	

Analysis: The error makes sense in the story because there are pictures of tigers and lions on the page. The intended message is the same. It does sound right. It does not look similar.

Structure Cues

The structure of the text is an acceptable English language construction.

Ask: Is the error constructed correctly?

Text	Errors		Cues Used	
✓ ✓ ✓ play ✓ ✓ I like to eat ice cream.	E	SC	E	SC
	1		S	

Analysis: This is an acceptable English language construction up to and including the error. It does not look right.

© Macmillan/McGraw-Hill

Visual Cues

The visual cues in the text are the visual appearance of the letters and the words.

Ask: Does the error look like the word in the text?

Text		Errors		Cues Used	
✓ ✓ ✓ ✓ stay ✓ ✓ ✓ I like to see stars in the sky.		E	SC	E	SC
		1		V	

Analysis: The error looks similar. It does not sound right. It does not make sense.

Self-Corrections

In analyzing a Running Record, it is important not only to determine what cues were being used when an error was made, but also what cues were being used when a self-correction was made.

Ask: What probably caused the student to self-correct this error?

Text		Errors		Cues Used	
✓ ✓ ✓ ✓ ✓ house/S ✓ ✓ We went over to their home for dinner.		E	SC	E	SC
			1	SV	V

Analysis: The error does sound right. It does look similar.

Self-Correction Analysis: The student most likely attended to the final consonant. Therefore, a visual cue was used. Without awareness of any other text or the actual meaning of the story, the use of meaning cues is difficult to determine.

© Macmillan/McGraw-Hill

Determining Error Rate and Reading Accuracy Percentage

To determine a student's error rate, divide the total number of words read by the total number of errors made. Take this number and convert it into a ratio. For example, a student who read a total of 60 words and made four errors has an error rate of 1:15. The student made one error for every 15 words read. To determine a student's reading accuracy percentage, we have provided a Conversion Table on page 7 that easily converts a student's error rate into a reading accuracy percentage. It is helpful to keep this chart handy when assessing students.

Look at the table on page 7. A student who has an error rate of 1:15 reads with a 93% reading accuracy percentage.

Formula for Error Rate

$$\text{Error Rate 1:} \frac{\text{Running Words}}{\text{Errors}} ^ *$$

*Use the ratio and refer to the Conversion Table on page 7 to get a reading accuracy percentage.

Determine the reading accuracy percentage to identify a student's reading level:

- 95%–100% is an independent reading level
- 90%–94% is an instructional reading level
- 89% and below is a frustrational reading level

Determining Self-Correction Rate

Self-corrections are positive reading behaviors. To determine a student's self-correction rate, add the number of errors and the number of self-corrections. Then divide this total by the number of self-corrections. This will give you a ratio.

Self-Correction Rate

$$\text{Self-Correction Rate 1:} \frac{\text{Errors + Self-Corrections}}{\text{Self-Corrections}}$$

Example: The student made ten errors and self-corrected five of them.

$$1:\frac{10 + 5}{5} = 3 \quad 1:3 = \text{Self-Correction Rate}^*$$

*The self-correction rate is expressed as 1:3. This means that the student corrects one out of every three errors. If a student is self-correcting at a rate of 1:3 or less, this indicates that she or he is self-monitoring her or his reading. This is an acceptable self-correction rate.

© Macmillan/McGraw-Hill

Conversion Table

The Conversion Table provides you with a fast conversion from an Error Rate to a Reading Accuracy Percentage.

CONVERSION TABLE

Error Rate	Reading Accuracy Percentage	Reading Level
1:200	99.5	
1:100	99	
1: 50	98	Independent Level: Appropriate for Independent Reading
1: 35	97	
1: 25	96	
1: 20	95	
1: 17	94	
1: 14	93	
1: 12.5	92	Instructional Level: Appropriate for Guided Reading
1: 11.75	91	
1: 10	90	
1: 9	89	
1: 8	87.5	
1: 7	85.5	
1: 6	83	
1: 5	80	Frustrational Level: Appropriate for Read Alouds
1: 4	75	
1: 3	66	
1: 2	50	

© Macmillan/McGraw-Hill

Procedure for Scoring Running Records

1. Count the total number of scorable errors as outlined in numbers 1–4 and 7 below. Write the total number of errors in the space indicated on the recording sheet. Insertions, substitutions, words told to the student by the teacher, and omissions are counted as errors at each occurrence. Words that are self-corrected and repeated are not errors.

2. If a student mispronounces a proper name, count it as one error for the entire passage, even if the student mispronounces the same name while reading the passage.

Code for Marking Word Recognition Errors

Each word recognition error is counted as one error. Never count more than one error on any one word.

Examples	**Marking Word Recognition Errors**
✓ ✓ ✓ The baby cried	1. Put a check mark over words read correctly.
✓ ✓ My friend (went)	2. Circle omissions.
✓ eats ✓ ✓ He ate the pie	3. Draw a line above words that are read with substitutions. Write the substitution above the line.
✓ T ✓ Why are you	4. Place a T above a word that you need to tell student.
✓ eating R dinner	5. Place an R next to a word the student repeats.
✓ ✓ ✓ See /S a kind person. She	6. Place the student's initial response and an S above a word that is self-corrected. Note: Do not score as an error.
✓ ✓ a (red) apple	7. Use parentheses ( ) to enclose a word that is inserted.

© Macmillan/McGraw-Hill

Example of a Passage with Coded Word Recognition Errors

✓   ✓   ✓ ✓   ✓ ✓ get ✓ ✓   ✓ ✓   ✓   ✓

Pam went to the store to buy a cake for the surprise party.

✓   ✓   ✓ ✓   ✓   ✓   T

The cake was for her mom's birthday.

✓   ✓ ✓   T   ✓ ✓   ✓   likes/S   ch/S

Pam got a chocolate cake. Her R mom (really) loves chocolate.

Here is what the teacher heard as the student read the passage. The words in italics are the actual words that the student read.

"Pam went to get a cake for the surprise party. The cake was for her mom's birthday.

Pam got a (after five seconds the teacher produced "chocolate") *cake. Her...Her mom really likes... loves ch...ch...chocolate."*

The student made four mistakes that are scored as errors:

(1) *get* substituted for *buy*
(2) *birthday* pronounced by the teacher
(3) *chocolate* pronounced by the teacher
(4) *really* inserted

The self-correction for *ch* is not counted as an error.
The self-correction for *loves* is not counted as an error.
The repetition for *her* is not counted as an error.

This text is at the frustrational level for this student.

© Macmillan/McGraw-Hill

Running Record

Level: _____

Name: _____   Age: _____   RW: _____

Text: _____   Reading Accuracy Percentage: _____

Circle Reading Level: Independent   Instructional   Frustrational   SC Rate: _____

	E	SC	MSV(E)	MSV(SC)
TOTAL				

© Macmillan/McGraw-Hill

Key: **RW**=Running Words   **SC**=Self-Correction   **E**=Errors

Three Options for Checking Comprehension

After you have completed the Running Record, you need to check the student's comprehension. Use this information in conjunction with the student's reading accuracy percentage to determine the student's true instructional level. There are three options for assessing comprehension:

- Retelling; scored with a Retelling Rubric on a scale of 1–4
- Two comprehension questions
- Graphic organizer

Retelling

Retelling incorporates several research-based strategies recommended by the National Reading Panel. As students retell, they organize their thinking and demonstrate higher level reasoning. Encourage students to retell the entire story or passage as if they are telling it to a friend.

Use the following rubric to evaluate your students' retellings:

☐ **4.** Accurate information, told in sequence, very detailed.

☐ **3.** Accurate information, adequate detail and description.

☐ **2.** Limited information, few if any details.

☐ **1.** Incorrect information, little or no understanding.

Comprehension Questions

There is an explicit and implicit comprehension question for each booklet and passage. The questions appear on the back of the booklets and on the recording forms. The student is not required to read the questions. Record responses on the form, then evaluate the depth, detail, and accuracy of each response.

Graphic Organizers

There are eight graphic organizers located on **pages 120–127** for you to choose from, or use one of your own. All of these are from the **Macmillan/McGraw-Hill Treasures** program.

© Macmillan/McGraw-Hill

This is a story about a boy who saved his town from a dragon.

Peter and the Dragon
by Ann Langran

A long time ago, in a land far away, there lived a dragon. He frightened all the people who lived in the town. Every time he was hungry, someone would disappear! The king offered a reward of one hundred bags of gold to anybody brave enough to make the dragon stop snacking on people.

Peter was the son of the best baker in the land. His job was to take cakes to the king's palace. Peter spent many hours wishing he was brave enough to face the dragon. One day, when he was planning what he could do with one hundred bags of gold, he got lost on his way to the palace. Without warning, he felt the ground tremble beneath him and he heard the roar of a terrible beast. **131 words**

There was the dragon showing his large teeth. Peter did not feel very brave. But he gathered up his courage and said, "Please don't eat me. My father is the best pastry cook in the whole land!" The dragon answered with a roar. "I can bring you cakes for the rest of your life!" cried Peter.

The dragon stopped in the middle of a roar. "Can you bring me those little cakes with pink icing?" he asked.

The next day, Peter returned with his father's best cakes. From then on the dragon lost his taste for people and was happy to eat cakes every day. Peter was happy with one hundred bags of gold!

Comprehension Check

1. What was Peter's problem in this story?

2. How did Peter solve his problem?

© Macmillan/McGraw-Hill

This is a passage about how glass is made.

Glassblowing
by Jenny Plastow

Everywhere in the world people make lovely objects out of glass. Glass can be clear or colored, thick or thin. It can be made by machine or by hand.

Today you find glass used in many places and for many objects. Glass is used to make more than 50,000 products! You find glass in your home, in your school, and in your car. Glass is used for windows and mirrors and televisions. It is made into dishes, bowls, and cups. It is crafted into beautiful jewelry.

Glass is made from sand which is heated until it melts and becomes a clear liquid. Then a glassblower dips a tube called a blowpipe into this liquid glass so that a bead forms on the end. Then he blows steadily into the tube until the bead becomes a hollow balloon. **137 words**

Now the glassblower can bend and shape the soft glass balloon to create objects. He can roll and stretch the glass. He puts it on a cold, steel bench called an anvil. Then he uses scissors and tweezers to make the shape he wants to make. As the glass cools it is wiped with a wet leather cloth. Finally, it is left standing to become cold, smooth, and hard.

How long does glass last? Glass objects can last for a very long time. People who study objects from the past often find glass cups and jewelry that were made hundreds of years ago.

Comprehension Check

1. What steps does a glassblower take to make glass?

2. How did glassblowers probably get their name?

© Macmillan/McGraw-Hill

This is a story about a boy who saw a strange light outside his window.

Night Light
by Jenny Plastow

Max woke up suddenly. What was that sound? He kept perfectly still and listened, but he could not hear anything else. Then he noticed a beam of light move slowly across his bedroom floor, as if a car with its headlights on was passing the window. Only the light was green. Then the beam swept back, from the opposite direction. How could it be car headlights? Max lived in an apartment and his room was on the eighteenth floor.

Max leapt out of bed and ran to the window to look out. Floating in the air was an oval-shaped, silver spaceship with green lights glowing from its surface. At one end was a headlight shining toward his window. **118 words**

As he stared without moving, Max thought he could see the shape of a small creature guiding the light toward him. The creature had large round pale eyes and when Max looked at him, their eyes met.

For a long, quiet moment the two stared at each other. Then suddenly the light went out and Max found himself looking out over the familiar view of the city. Lights twinkled below and the sound of late-night traffic rose to his ears.

No spaceship, no light, no little person. But as Max climbed slowly back into his bed, he knew what he had seen.

Comprehension Check

1. What caused Max to wake up?

2. Do you think what Max saw could be real? Why?

© Macmillan/McGraw-Hill

This is a passage about staying fit.

Staying Fit
by Maggie Threadingham

Long ago, keeping fit was not a problem for most people. They walked or rode every day as part of their work. Some people had jobs digging, pushing, lifting, or carrying heavy things. This hard work helped to keep people fit. But then times changed. Today fewer people have hard physical jobs. They drive to work in cars or travel on buses, subways, or trains. Many sit at a table or a desk to do their work and do not have an opportunity to walk or run much. As daily life no longer keeps them fit, lots of people turn to sports instead.
103 words

There are many sports to choose from if you want to keep fit. But when people play a sport they often look for more than just physical fitness. They choose a sport they can play with friends or one that they really enjoy.

Some sports, like soccer, are played with a team that competes with other teams. Playing in a team helps players improve their game. Some teams are made up of five or nine players, but others, like tennis or golf, have one to four players on a team. People who choose these kinds of sports have to practice on their own to get better.

There are still other sports, like swimming, running, skating, and yoga, that people can do alone. Some people enjoy working out in a gym by themselves or with a friend. How would you choose to stay physically fit?

Comprehension Check

1. How are jobs different today than they were in the past?

2. What are two ways people can stay fit?

© Macmillan/McGraw-Hill

This is a story about a girl who liked to hide in an old barn.

The Old Barn
by Jenny Plastow

Nobody ever used the deserted barn in the corner of the open field. In fact, since it seemed so old and broken down, no one even went near it. But it was where Sonia liked to go whenever she felt angry and confused. When she was troubled or unhappy she wanted to be alone and the barn was the best place she knew for being alone.

Sonia went through the big door into the coolness of the barn. Once inside, she felt calm and safe. It was totally silent in the dark building; nobody shouted or yelled, and no little brothers whined or teased. Sonia climbed up the steep ladder to the hayloft. As soon as she reached the top she started to feel better. In a corner of the hayloft she had hidden some books and a container filled with cookies. She settled down for a long, peaceful read. **150 words**

After a while, Sonia grew calm. She was surprised to realize that she felt lonely for the company of her noisy family. Carefully, she put the lid back on the cookies, and marked her place in her book. Then she left the barn and ran home.

Her mom looked up as she walked in. "Hi Mom," said Sonia. "Sorry I gave you such a hard time before. I guess that I was feeling uncomfortable." Mom moved over to make room for Sonia on the couch and said, "Let's talk."

Comprehension Check

1. What made Sonia go to the old barn?

2. What do you think Sonia and her mother talked about back home?

© Macmillan/McGraw-Hill

This is a passage about finding ways to control feelings of anger.

Keeping It Under Control
by Bobbie Neate

We all experience different feelings every day. Some feelings are very enjoyable, like happiness and excitement. Other feelings are not so wonderful. Feeling let down or sad are feelings that are not easy to deal with. Feeling alone can be hard. Probably the most difficult feeling to face is the feeling of anger.

We get angry when we see someone else being hurt or when things happen that do not seem fair or just. Sometimes not getting something we have worked hard for can make us angry. When these things happen, anger can build up inside. This anger stops us from thinking clearly or knowing the right way to act. **110 words**

When you feel this way, it is a good idea to try to tell someone. At first you may not be able to explain how you feel very well. You might not find the right words right away. But you should try. Remember to speak clearly and calmly, and not to shout.

Once someone else knows how you feel, and starts to listen, it gets easier to explain why you feel angry. Using words to express how you feel may also help you know what makes you angry. That will help you do something about the situation. You can start to work out the best way to deal with the anger.

Comprehension Check

1. What are some events that can cause anger?

2. What steps can you take when you feel angry?

© Macmillan/McGraw-Hill

This is a story about twins who are very different.

Lucy and Tom
by Emilia Nueva

Most twins have a lot in common. After all, they grow up in the same house and have the same parents and do many things together. But there are some twins who are different in almost every way.

Lucy Layman cares more about sports than anything else. She is an athlete who always wants to be outside playing some sport. She wins every running race she enters and sets records for high jumps and other track events. She can hit more balls on the tennis court than anyone else in her town. Most of all, Lucy loves to play soccer. She practices the game whenever she has a chance and she is an unbeatable force on the soccer field. **119 words**

Tom Layman is tall and thin and could be good at sports, but he is just not interested. He would rather read or work on his computer. When he goes to one of Lucy's sporting events, he usually brings along a book. While she is out practicing, he stays home and takes a machine apart and then puts it back together. Tom's idea of a fun afternoon is a trip to the library to read about the latest developments in science and technology.

There is one thing that Tom and Lucy definitely do share. They are proud of each other. Tom thinks that Lucy's athletic talent is awesome and is going to take her far. Lucy tells everyone she knows how good Tom is with computers. These twins do have something in common!

Comprehension Check

1. How are Lucy and Tom different? How are they the same?

2. What do you think will happen to the twins when they grow up?

© Macmillan/McGraw-Hill

This is a passage about earthquakes.

Earthquake!
by Rashib Haver

Early in the morning of January, in 1994, disaster struck the city of Los Angeles. An earthquake shook the land. Bridges collapsed, buildings fell, and streets crumbled to dust. Thousands of people were left homeless. Three major highways were closed. It was one of the worse natural disasters in the history of the United States.

The Los Angeles area has many fault lines, large cracks in Earth's crust at or below the surface. During an earthquake, blocks of crust move past each other at these lines. Sometimes the ground moves back and forth during an earthquake. At other times it moves up and down. **104 words**

What makes the damage of an earthquake so severe? Strong tremors, or shaking movements, can cause ground to give away. Land breaks apart, landslides occur, buildings fall. Fires start when gas or electrical wiring is damaged. Things get worse when firefighters are unable to reach damaged areas to put fires out.

In 1994 California already had many building codes to protect structures during earthquakes. After the earthquake engineers who design bridges and buildings went right to work. They were surprised to learn that many buildings and bridges had not held up as well as they expected them to. New and stronger building codes were written and enforced. The lessons they learned will help save lives.

Comprehension Check

1. What happens to the earth during an earthquake?

2. Why do earthquakes cause so much damage?

© Macmillan/McGraw-Hill

This is a story about a desert island.

Island of Purple Fruit
by Bobbie Neate

Long ago a ship was exploring the South Seas, hoping to discover treasure. When a terrible storm wrecked the ship, Horace was the only survivor. He washed ashore on a desert island, and for the first few days, Horace remained where he had landed on the beach. All Horace could think about was being rescued. He was always looking out at the sea, hoping to catch a glimpse of a ship sailing over the horizon.

After three days, though, Horace was so hungry that he decided he had to leave the beach and hunt for food. Horace searched the island from end to end but all he could find was a strange purple fruit that grew at the top of very tall trees. But Horace was worried about spending too much time away from the beach, so he quickly headed back to the shore. For the next few days, Horace sat and stared out at the sea, but he was growing hungrier and hungrier. **164 words**

Finally, Horace decided that he had to climb one of the trees with the purple fruit. So he scaled one of the very tall trees and picked as much fruit as he could. When Horace took a bite of the fruit, it tasted sweet and delicious. It was the best fruit he had ever eaten.

After he ate, Horace immediately fell asleep and dreamed of a large ship approaching the island. Then Horace heard voices and felt someone shaking him. It was not a dream, and Horace's rescue ship was real. The sailors helped him gather as much of the purple fruit as they could carry. Horace looked forward to going home and sharing his sweet treasure.

Comprehension Check

1. What happened after Horace ate the purple fruit?

2. Why was Horace afraid at first to climb the tree and get the purple fruit?

© Macmillan/McGraw-Hill

This is a time line about a famous explorer.

Christopher Columbus
by Maggie Threadingham

1451

Christopher Columbus is born in Genoa, Italy.

1465

Columbus becomes a sailor and takes his first voyage. He also studies navigation and mapmaking.

1481

Columbus believes he can find a quicker route to the Far East if he sails west across the Atlantic Ocean, but he needs money to fund his expedition.

1492

Queen Isabella and King Ferdinand of Spain agree to pay for the trip. On August 3rd, Columbus sets sail with three ships. On October 12th, they land on a small island. Columbus names it San Salvador. He also lands on what is today the Dominican Republic and calls it Hispaniola. **104 words**

1493

In October, Columbus embarks on his second expedition. He establishes a colony on Hispaniola.

1498

Columbus makes a third voyage to the New World, this time reaching the coast of South America.

1502

On his last trip to the New World, Columbus sails along the coast of Central America. He is shipwrecked on the island of Jamaica for many months.

1506

Columbus dies in Spain.

Comprehension Check

1. Why did Columbus sail west?

2. What did Columbus need to do before his expedition?

© Macmillan/McGraw-Hill

This is a story about a friendship between a boy and a falcon.

Ping and the Falcon
by Bobbie Neate

In Ancient China there lived a peasant boy named Ping. Thirteen-year-old Ping was responsible for taking care of his father's goats. Ping spent every day in the fields tending to the goats. Ping found the work challenging but he was also lonely and longed for a friend.

One sweltering summer day, as Ping was watching the goats, a beautiful falcon descended from the sky. With its wings stretched wide, the falcon circled over the boy, each time coming lower and lower. Ping waved to the falcon, and the falcon swooped down and landed on a boulder near the boy.

After that day, the falcon visited Ping often and the boy and the falcon became friends. Ping named the great bird Chunwin. **121 words**

Chunwin was an amazing bird because he could do tricks without any training. He just listened to Ping and did exactly what the boy said.

Later that year, Ping heard that China was under attack by an invading army. China needed to protect its land against its enemies, so the army sent messenger pigeons into the villages to search for people willing to become soldiers. But the pigeons were stopped by the enemy's hawks.

Ping wanted to help his country, so he told Chunwin to find the enemy's hawks and lead them away. Chunwin did as he was told. Chunwin led the hawks into the mountains and deep into a cave, where they all disappeared. Ping heard about the mysterious disappearance of the hawks. Ping never saw Chunwin again, but told everyone about the falcon's bravery and what the great bird had done.

Comprehension Check

1. In what way was Ping a hero in this story?

2. How did Chunwin show his loyalty to Ping?

© Macmillan/McGraw-Hill

This is a passage about Madrid, Spain.

Madrid

by Ann Langran

Location

Spain is located in the southwest corner of
Europe, across the Atlantic Ocean from the
United States. Madrid is Spain's capital,
and is in the center of the country. The
city is a connecting point to all parts of
Spain. The city's two towers are called the
Gateway to Europe.

Artistic Center

For years Madrid's outdoor restaurants
have been a meeting place for students,
artists, and writers. Madrid is an important cultural center.
It has many museums, gardens, and theaters. The Prado, the
largest art museum in the world, is located here. **93 words**

Madrid in Numbers

Population: 3 million
Land area: 236 square miles (about the size of Oregon)
Temperature: 42 degrees (in January) and 75 degrees
(in July)

Major Products

Olives, grapes, beets, and fish. Madrid has the world's
second-largest fish market.

Major Industries

Textiles, tourism, shipbuilding, and pottery making

Did You Know?

- Madrid is Europe's highest city at 2,100 feet.
- At midnight on New Year's Eve, people eat 12 grapes to the
  beat of the clock. This is supposed to bring them good luck.

Comprehension Check

1. What are two facts you learned about Madrid?

2. Why do you think the towers are called the Gateway to Europe?

© Macmillan/McGraw-Hill

This is a tale about an ancient creature.

The Minotaur
by Jenny Plastow

The Minotaur, a ferocious creature that was half bull and half man, was kept in a labyrinth under the palace of King Minos. Every year seven young people from Athens were sacrificed to the Minotaur.

One year brave Theseus volunteered to be one of the Minotaur's victims. Theseus had slain many monsters before and he was determined to kill the Minotaur.

Ariadne, the daughter of Minos, devised a plan to help Theseus escape. At the entrance to the labyrinth, Ariadne tied the end of a ball of thread to the doorway and then gave the ball of thread to Theseus. **100 words**

"What is that for?" asked Theseus.

"Even if you defeat the monster, you will be wandering in the maze," said Ariadne. "The ball of thread will help you find your way back. Unwind the thread as you go, then you will be able to retrace your steps."

Theseus could hear the Minotaur roaring the moment he stepped into the maze. Suddenly, the Minotaur was upon him. It was a difficult fight but Theseus managed to defeat the Minotaur. Then he carefully wound up the ball of thread that guided him back through the maze.

Ariadne was waiting for him by the doorway.

"You will be in danger for helping me," Theseus said to her. "Come with me!"

Comprehension Check

1. Why did Ariadne give Theseus the ball of thread?

2. Why might Ariadne be in danger at the end of the story?

Pronunciation Key:

'Mĭ-nə-tor   'Mī-nəs   A-rē-'ad-nē   'Thē-sē-əs

© Macmillan/McGraw-Hill

This passage explains the meaning of Independence Day.

Independence Day
by Jenny Plastow

In the seventeenth century, Britain had thirteen colonies in North America. Britain ruled the colonies and the American colonies grew and prospered.

The relationship between Britain and the colonists began to change after the French and Indian War. The war broke out because France claimed land in North America that Britain wanted. Britain won the war.

However, the war was expensive and Britain thought that the American colonists should help pay for it. So in 1765 the British passed the Stamp Act, which was a tax on many goods. In 1773, the British started to tax tea and then enacted other laws that the colonists thought were unfair. These events led to the start of the American Revolution in 1775. **120 words**

In June of 1776, members of the Continental Congress met in Philadelphia. They decided it was time to officially declare America's independence.

Thomas Jefferson was asked to write the declaration. In it, Jefferson described the rights that every man was entitled to, including "life, liberty, and the pursuit of happiness." He listed all of the colonists' grievances with Britain. Finally, he declared that the colonies were free and independent states.

On July 4, 1776, the Declaration of Independence was approved by Congress.

The war with Britain didn't end until 1781, but every July 4, the United States celebrates Independence Day.

Comprehension Check

1. What were some of the events that led up to the American Revolution?

2. Why is the Declaration of Independence an important document in American History?

© Macmillan/McGraw-Hill

This is a story about a boy overcoming his challenges.

Danny's Challenge
by Bobbie Neate

The man at the reception desk looked doubtful when Danny wanted to sign up to climb and rappel the gym's rock wall. But Dad was insistent as he looked the man firmly in the eye. "My son wishes to try this sport," he said. The man shrugged his shoulders and said, "Okay. Sign here."

Danny had one leg shorter than the other as a result of an accident when he was younger. Danny didn't walk very evenly, but the muscles in his legs were extremely strong. He desperately wanted to try climbing the rock wall and rappelling down. It was important that he find a sport that he could participate in. He wanted to be like everyone else. **118 words**

First, Danny had to take a class in proper procedures for climbing and rappelling. He practiced wearing the harness and working the ropes. He was so excited he could hardly wait!

Finally his chance arrived, and Danny could feel everyone's eyes on him as the ropes and harness were fastened around him. When the harness was on tight, he felt himself being lifted up and for a moment he too wondered whether he could do this.

It was fantastic! Way up high, supported by strong ropes, traveling down in great leaps and bounds, Danny felt as free as a bird. He wished the wall were a hundred times as high, and the experience a hundred times as long. But all too soon he reached the bottom and helpful hands were loosening his harness. He set off toward his dad, unable to stop smiling or conceal his feeling of personal success.

"Incredible" he shouted as his dad, grinning, came within hearing. "Astonishing! When can I do it again, Dad?"

Comprehension Check

1. Why did Danny's father insist that his son sign up?

2. Why do you think it was important for Danny to do this?

© Macmillan/McGraw-Hill

This passage explains what tectonic plates are.

Tectonic Plates

by Jenny Plastow

Earth's crust is broken up into large sections called tectonic plates, which float on molten rock inside the earth. The plates fit together like the pieces in a puzzle but they are constantly moving.

Tectonic plates move in many different ways. Sometimes two plates pull apart, causing rifts and valleys, while other plates crash into each other, forming mountains. Some plates slide past each other. The places where the edges of the plates meet, or where there are cracks in the earth's surface, are called faults.

Many of earth's features were formed by the movement of the tectonic plates. The Himalaya Mountains were created when the India Plate crashed into the Asia Plate. The Mid-Atlantic Ridge was formed by two plates pulling apart. Molten rock from inside the earth seeped out, forming the submerged mountain range. **136 words**

Most earthquakes and volcanoes happen along the plate boundaries. Earthquakes happen most frequently in places where two plates are sliding past each other. California has experienced many earthquakes because it is on the boundary of the Pacific Plate, which is moving northwest, and the North American plate, which is moving in a southerly direction.

Volcanoes often form in places where oceanic and continental plates converge, or meet. For example, there are many active volcanoes around the edges of the Pacific Plate, in an area that is called the Ring of Fire. Volcanoes form when magma, or molten rock, from deep inside the earth erupts through the earth's crust.

Comprehension Check

1. Why has California experienced earthquakes?

2. Why do you think the area around the Pacific Plate is called the Ring of Fire?

© Macmillan/McGraw-Hill

Running Record

Level: _Rebus_

Name: _____   Age: _____   RW: _25_

Text: _My Family_____   Reading Accuracy Percentage: _____

Circle Reading Level: Independent   Instructional   Frustrational   SC Rate: _____

		E	SC	MSV(E)	MSV(SC)
This is a story about a family.					
Here is my house.					
Here is my Mom.					
Here is my Grandma.					
Here is my baby.					
Here is my dog.					
And here is my family!					
	TOTAL				

Key: RW=Running Words   **SC**=Self-Correction   **E**=Errors

© Macmillan/McGraw-Hill

Running Record

Level <u>Rebus</u>

Name _____ Date _____

Text <u>My Family</u>

Retelling Rubric

☐ **4** Accurate information, told in sequence, very detailed.

☐ **3** Accurate information, adequate detail and description.

☐ **2** Limited information, few if any details.

☐ **1** Incorrect information, little or no understanding.

Graphic Organizer: _____

Comprehension Check

1. What is the story about?

Student Response: _____

2. Why is the boy chasing the dog?

Student Response: _____

Reading Level

Error Rate $1 : \dfrac{(RW)}{(E)}$ _____ *

*Use the ratio and refer to the Conversion Table on page 7 to get a **reading accuracy percentage.**

Reading Accuracy Percentage: _____ %

Self-Correction Rate $1 : \dfrac{(E) + (SC)}{(SC)}$

Observed Reading Behaviors

- moves left to right on one line of text   ☐
- demonstrates control of one to one matching   ☐
- rereads to confirm and search for meaning   ☐
- uses intonation and expression   ☐
- uses phrasing   ☐
- uses picture cues to confirm context and visual cues ☐

At points of difficulty, the student will _____

_____

© Macmillan/McGraw-Hill

Running Record

Level: _____Rebus_____

Name: _____ Age: _____ RW: __24__

Text: __Pets_____ Reading Accuracy Percentage: _____

Circle Reading Level: Independent Instructional Frustrational SC Rate: _____

	E	SC	MSV(E)	MSV(SC)
This book is all about pets.				
This is a dog.				
This is a cat.				
This is a bunny.				
This is a fish.				
This is a bird.				
This is a turtle.				
TOTAL				

Key: **RW**=Running Words **SC**=Self-Correction **E**=Errors

© Macmillan/McGraw-Hill

Running Record

Level <u>Rebus</u>

Name _____ Date _____

Text <u>Pets</u>

Retelling Rubric

☐ **4** Accurate information, told in sequence, very detailed.

☐ **3** Accurate information, adequate detail and description.

☐ **2** Limited information, few if any details.

☐ **1** Incorrect information, little or no understanding.

Graphic Organizer: _____

Comprehension Check

1. Which pets have fur?

Student Response: _____

2. Which pet can live in water?

Student Response: _____

Reading Level

Error Rate $1 : \dfrac{(RW)}{(E)}$ *

*Use the ratio and refer to the Conversion Table on page 7 to get a **reading accuracy percentage.**

Reading Accuracy Percentage: _____ %

Self-Correction Rate $1 : \dfrac{(E) + (SC)}{(SC)}$

Observed Reading Behaviors

- moves left to right on one line of text   ☐
- demonstrates control of one to one matching   ☐
- rereads to confirm and search for meaning   ☐
- uses intonation and expression   ☐
- uses phrasing   ☐
- uses picture cues to confirm context and visual cues   ☐

At points of difficulty, the student will _____

© Macmillan/McGraw-Hill

Running Record

Level: __1__

Name: _____

Age: _____   RW: __24__

Text: __Sam at School_____

Reading Accuracy Percentage: _____

Circle Reading Level: Independent   Instructional   Frustrational

SC Rate: _____

	E	SC	MSV(E)	MSV(SC)
This is a story about Sam at school.				
I have a chair.				
I have a desk.				
I have a book.				
I have a pencil.				
I have a job.				
I have a bag.				
TOTAL				

Key: RW=Running Words   **SC**=Self-Correction   **E**=Errors

© Macmillan/McGraw-Hill

Running Record

Level __1__

Name _____   Date _____

Text __Sam at School__ _____

Retelling Rubric

☐ **4** Accurate information, told in sequence, very detailed.

☐ **3** Accurate information, adequate detail and description.

☐ **2** Limited information, few if any details.

☐ **1** Incorrect information, little or no understanding.

Graphic Organizer: _____

Comprehension Check

1. Where is Sam?

Student Response: _____

2. What is Sam doing in the story?

Student Response: _____

Reading Level

Error Rate $1 : \dfrac{(RW)}{(E)}$ ____ *

*Use the ratio and refer to the Conversion Table on page 7 to get a **reading accuracy percentage.**

Reading Accuracy Percentage: _____ %

Self-Correction Rate $1 : \dfrac{(E) + (SC)}{(SC)}$

Observed Reading Behaviors

• moves left to right on one line of text   ☐

• demonstrates control of one to one matching   ☐

• rereads to confirm and search for meaning   ☐

• uses intonation and expression   ☐

• uses phrasing   ☐

• uses picture cues to confirm context and visual cues ☐

At points of difficulty, the student will _____

© Macmillan/McGraw-Hill

Running Record

Level: 1

Name: _____

Age: _____ RW: 18

Text: See Me! _____

Reading Accuracy Percentage: _____

Circle Reading Level: Independent   Instructional   Frustrational   SC Rate: _____

	E	SC	MSV(E)	MSV(SC)
This book is about the parts of your body.				
See my hands.				
See my feet.				
See my eyes.				
See my nose.				
See my ears.				
See my face!				
TOTAL				

© Macmillan/McGraw-Hill

Key: RW=Running Words   **SC**=Self-Correction   **E**=Errors

Running Record

Name _____ Date _____

Text See Me! _____

Retelling Rubric

☐ **4** Accurate information, told in sequence, very detailed.

☐ **3** Accurate information, adequate detail and description.

☐ **2** Limited information, few if any details.

☐ **1** Incorrect information, little or no understanding.

Graphic Organizer: _____

Comprehension Check

1. What is this story about?

Student Response: _____

2. Name the parts of your body.

Student Response: _____

Reading Level

Error Rate $1 : \dfrac{(RW)}{(E)}$ _____ *

*Use the ratio and refer to the Conversion Table on page 7 to get a **reading accuracy percentage.**

Reading Accuracy Percentage: _____ %

Self-Correction Rate $1 : \dfrac{(E) + (SC)}{(SC)}$

Observed Reading Behaviors

- moves left to right on one line of text ☐
- demonstrates control of one to one matching ☐
- rereads to confirm and search for meaning ☐
- uses intonation and expression ☐
- uses phrasing ☐
- uses picture cues to confirm context and visual cues ☐

At points of difficulty, the student will _____

_____

© Macmillan/McGraw-Hill

Running Record

Level: 2

Name: _____

Age: _____   RW: 27

Text: Pat at the Park

Reading Accuracy Percentage: _____

Circle Reading Level: Independent   Instructional   Frustrational

SC Rate: _____

	E	SC	MSV(E)	MSV(SC)
This story is about playing in the park.				
Look at Pat go up.				
Look at Pat go down.				
Look at Pat go in.				
Look at Pat eat.				
Look at Pat play.				
Look at Pat go!				
TOTAL				

Key: RW=Running Words   **SC**=Self-Correction   **E**=Errors

© Macmillan/McGraw-Hill

Running Record

Level 2

Name _____ Date _____

Text __Pat at the Park__

Retelling Rubric

☐ **4** Accurate information, told in sequence, very detailed.

☐ **3** Accurate information, adequate detail and description.

☐ **2** Limited information, few if any details.

☐ **1** Incorrect information, little or no understanding.

Graphic Organizer: _____

Comprehension Check

1. Where is Pat?

Student Response: _____

2. What does Pat do at the park?

Student Response: _____

Reading Level

Error Rate $1 : \dfrac{(RW)}{(E)}$ *

*Use the ratio and refer to the Conversion Table on page 7 to get a **reading accuracy percentage.**

Reading Accuracy Percentage: _____ %

Self-Correction Rate $1 : \dfrac{(E) + (SC)}{(SC)}$

Observed Reading Behaviors

- moves left to right on one line of text ☐
- demonstrates control of one to one matching ☐
- rereads to confirm and search for meaning ☐
- uses intonation and expression ☐
- uses phrasing ☐
- uses picture cues to confirm context and visual cues ☐

At points of difficulty, the student will _____

_____

© Macmillan/McGraw-Hill

Running Record

Level: 2

Name: _____

Age: _____ RW: 23

Text: Cats

Reading Accuracy Percentage: _____

Circle Reading Level: Independent   Instructional   Frustrational   SC Rate: _____

	E	SC	MSV(E)	MSV(SC)
This is a story about what cats like.				
Cats like to eat.				
Cats like to drink.				
Cats like to lick.				
Cats like to play.				
Cats like to sleep.				
Cats like me!				
TOTAL				

Key: RW=Running Words   **SC**=Self-Correction   **E**=Errors

© Macmillan/McGraw-Hill

Running Record

Name _____ Date _____

Text _Cats_____

Retelling Rubric

☐ **4** Accurate information, told in sequence, very detailed.

☐ **3** Accurate information, adequate detail and description.

☐ **2** Limited information, few if any details.

☐ **I** Incorrect information, little or no understanding.

Graphic Organizer: _____

Comprehension Check

1. What do cats like?

Student Response: _____

2. What can cats do?

Student Response: _____

Reading Level

Error Rate $1: \dfrac{(RW)}{(E)}$ *

*Use the ratio and refer to the Conversion Table on page 7 to get a **reading accuracy percentage.**

Reading Accuracy Percentage: _____ %

Self-Correction Rate $1: \dfrac{(E) + (SC)}{(SC)}$

Observed Reading Behaviors

- moves left to right on one line of text   ☐
- demonstrates control of one to one matching   ☐
- rereads to confirm and search for meaning   ☐
- uses intonation and expression   ☐
- uses phrasing   ☐
- uses picture cues to confirm context and visual cues   ☐

At points of difficulty, the student will _____

© Macmillan/McGraw-Hill

Running Record

Level: 3

Name: _____

Age: _____   RW: 53

Text: __Up and Down_____

Reading Accuracy Percentage: _____

Circle Reading Level: Independent   Instructional   Frustrational

SC Rate: _____

	E	SC	MSV(E)	MSV(SC)
This story is about a cat and a dog that are friends.				
Sam the cat liked to play.				
Rob the dog liked to play. Sam looked up.				
"Come down and play," said Sam to Rob.				
"Come up and play," said Rob to Sam.				
"I am going down," said Rob. "Here I am."				
"I am going up," said Sam. "Here I am."				
"Oh no!" they said.				
TOTAL				

Key: RW=Running Words   **SC**=Self-Correction   **E**=Errors

© Macmillan/McGraw-Hill

Running Record

Level _3_

Name _____ Date _____

Text _Up and Down_ _____

Retelling Rubric

☐ **4** Accurate information, told in sequence, very detailed.

☐ **3** Accurate information, adequate detail and description.

☐ **2** Limited information, few if any details.

☐ **I** Incorrect information, little or no understanding.

Graphic Organizer: _____

Comprehension Check

I. What is this story about?

Student Response: _____

2. What do Sam and Rob like to do together?

Student Response: _____

Reading Level

Error Rate $1: \dfrac{(RW)}{(E)}$ _____ *

*Use the ratio and refer to the Conversion Table on page 7 to get a **reading accuracy percentage.**

Reading Accuracy Percentage: _____ %

Self-Correction Rate $1: \dfrac{(E) + (SC)}{(SC)}$

Observed Reading Behaviors

- moves left to right on one line of text   ☐
- demonstrates control of one to one matching   ☐
- rereads to confirm and search for meaning   ☐
- uses intonation and expression   ☐
- uses phrasing   ☐
- uses picture cues to confirm context and visual cues ☐

At points of difficulty, the student will _____

© Macmillan/McGraw-Hill

Running Record

Level: 3

Name: _____   Age: _____   RW: 43

Text: Babies   Reading Accuracy Percentage: _____

Circle Reading Level: Independent   Instructional   Frustrational   SC Rate: _____

	E	SC	MSV(E)	MSV(SC)
This book is all about babies.				
This is a baby. He is looking.				
This is a baby. She is eating.				
This is a baby. He is crying.				
This is a baby. She is sitting.				
This is a baby. He is sleeping.				
This is a big baby. He is playing.				
TOTAL				

Key: RW=Running Words   **SC**=Self-Correction   **E**=Errors

© Macmillan/McGraw-Hill

Running Record

Level __3__

Name _____ Date _____

Text __Babies__ _____

Retelling Rubric

☐ **4** Accurate information, told in sequence, very detailed.

☐ **3** Accurate information, adequate detail and description.

☐ **2** Limited information, few if any details.

☐ **1** Incorrect information, little or no understanding.

Graphic Organizer: _____

Comprehension Check

1. What is this story about?

Student Response: _____

2. What are some things that babies can do?

Student Response: _____

Reading Level

Error Rate $1 : \dfrac{(RW)}{(E)}$ _____ *

*Use the ratio and refer to the Conversion Table on page 7 to get a **reading accuracy percentage.**

Reading Accuracy Percentage: _____ %

Self-Correction Rate $1 : \dfrac{(E) + (SC)}{(SC)}$

Observed Reading Behaviors

• moves left to right on one line of text ☐

• demonstrates control of one to one matching ☐

• rereads to confirm and search for meaning ☐

• uses intonation and expression ☐

• uses phrasing ☐

• uses picture cues to confirm context and visual cues ☐

At points of difficulty, the student will _____

_____

© Macmillan/McGraw-Hill

Running Record

Level: 4

Name: _____

Age: _____ RW: 72

Text: At the Pond

Reading Accuracy Percentage: _____

Circle Reading Level: Independent   Instructional   Frustrational   SC Rate: _____

	E	SC	MSV(E)	MSV(SC)
This story is about a day at the pond.				
Pam and Dad sat by the pretty pond. What did they see?				
"Look over there!" said Dad. "A little frog jumped out of the water."				
"Look over there!" said Pam. "The frog went back in the water."				
Dad said, "A frog can live in water. It can live on land, too."				
Dad said, "Look over there! This frog likes to jump."				
Pam said, "Look, Dad! This little frog jumped up on me!"				
TOTAL				

Key: **RW**=Running Words   **SC**=Self-Correction   **E**=Errors

© Macmillan/McGraw-Hill

Running Record

Level __4__

Name _____ Date _____

Text __At the Pond__

Retelling Rubric

☐ **4** Accurate information, told in sequence, very detailed.

☐ **3** Accurate information, adequate detail and description.

☐ **2** Limited information, few if any details.

☐ **I** Incorrect information, little or no understanding.

Graphic Organizer: _____

Comprehension Check

1. What did Pam and Dad see at the pond?

Student Response: _____

2. Where did the frog jump last?

Student Response: _____

Reading Level

Error Rate $1: \dfrac{(RW)}{(E)}$ _____ *

*Use the ratio and refer to the Conversion Table on page 7 to get a **reading accuracy percentage.**

Reading Accuracy Percentage: _____ %

Self-Correction Rate $1: \dfrac{(E) + (SC)}{(SC)}$ _____

Observed Reading Behaviors

- moves left to right on one line of text ☐
- demonstrates control of one to one matching ☐
- rereads to confirm and search for meaning ☐
- uses intonation and expression ☐
- uses phrasing ☐
- uses picture cues to confirm context and visual cues ☐

At points of difficulty, the student will _____

© Macmillan/McGraw-Hill

Running Record

Name: _____   Age: _____   Level: __4__

Text: __Who Works Here?__   RW: __70__

Reading Accuracy Percentage: _____

Circle Reading Level: Independent   Instructional   Frustrational   SC Rate: _____

	E	SC	MSV(E)	MSV(SC)
This book is about the jobs people do.				
A doctor has a job.				
She works to make				
us well.				
A teacher has a job.				
He teaches boys				
and girls.				
A farmer has a job.				
This farmer makes				
a stack of hay.				
A baker has a job.				
This baker makes				
a cake to eat.				
A clown has a job.				
He works with friends				
to make us happy.				
A painter has a job.				
She paints the room				
a new color.				
TOTAL				

Key: RW=Running Words   **SC**=Self-Correction   **E**=Errors

© Macmillan/McGraw-Hill

Running Record

Name _____   Date _____

Text _Who Works Here?_ _____

Retelling Rubric

☐ **4** Accurate information, told in sequence, very detailed.

☐ **3** Accurate information, adequate detail and description.

☐ **2** Limited information, few if any details.

☐ **I** Incorrect information, little or no understanding.

Graphic Organizer: _____

Comprehension Check

I. What are some jobs the people in this story have?

Student Response: _____

2. What job does a baker do? A doctor?

Student Response: _____

Reading Level

Error Rate I: $\dfrac{\text{(RW)}}{\text{(E)}}$ *

*Use the ratio and refer to the Conversion Table on page 7 to get a **reading accuracy percentage.**

Reading Accuracy Percentage: _____ %

Self-Correction Rate I: $\dfrac{\text{(E) + (SC)}}{\text{(SC)}}$

Observed Reading Behaviors

- moves left to right on one line of text ☐
- demonstrates control of one to one matching ☐
- rereads to confirm and search for meaning ☐
- uses intonation and expression ☐
- uses phrasing ☐
- uses picture cues to confirm context and visual cues ☐

At points of difficulty, the student will _____
_____

© Macmillan/McGraw-Hill

Running Record

Level: 6

Name: _____

Age: _____

RW: 92

Text: The Pig and the Fox

Reading Accuracy Percentage: _____

Circle Reading Level: Independent   Instructional   Frustrational   SC Rate: _____

	E	SC	MSV(E)	MSV(SC)
This is a story about a pig and a fox.				
There were two houses on the hill. Who lived there?				
The little pig lived in a brick home. He stayed inside and read books all day.				
The fox lived in a home made of sticks. He stayed inside and read newspapers all day.				
The fox said, "A stick home is best!" The little pig said, "A brick home is best!"				
A big wind came. It went around and around the two homes.				
Look what the wind did to the stick home! The walls all fell down. The brick home was the best!				
TOTAL				

Key: RW=Running Words   **SC**=Self-Correction   **E**=Errors

© Macmillan/McGraw-Hill

Running Record

Level _6_

Name _____   Date _____

Text _The Pig and the Fox_ _____

Retelling Rubric

☐ **4** Accurate information, told in sequence, very detailed.

☐ **3** Accurate information, adequate detail and description.

☐ **2** Limited information, few if any details.

☐ **1** Incorrect information, little or no understanding.

Graphic Organizer: _____

Comprehension Check

1. Which character lived in a stick house?

Student Response: _____

2. Why was a brick home the best?

Student Response: _____

Reading Level

Error Rate $1 : \dfrac{(RW)}{(E)}$ _____ *

*Use the ratio and refer to the Conversion Table on page 7 to get a **reading accuracy percentage.**

Reading Accuracy Percentage: _____ %

Self-Correction Rate $1 : \dfrac{(E) + (SC)}{(SC)}$

Observed Reading Behaviors

- moves left to right on one line of text ☐
- demonstrates control of one to one matching ☐
- rereads to confirm and search for meaning ☐
- uses intonation and expression ☐
- uses phrasing ☐
- uses picture cues to confirm context and visual cues ☐

At points of difficulty, the student will _____

_____

© Macmillan/McGraw-Hill

Running Record

Level: 6

Name: _____   Age: _____   RW: 90

Text: Grandmothers

Reading Accuracy Percentage: _____

Circle Reading Level: Independent   Instructional   Frustrational   SC Rate: _____

	E	SC	MSV(E)	MSV(SC)
This book shows you what grandmothers can do.				
What do grandmothers do?				
They can go places with				
their friends.				
Some grandmothers run fast to stay healthy.				
Running fast is a good way to exercise.				
This grandmother runs and jumps to stay				
healthy, too.				
Jumping and running is a good way to				
exercise.				
This grandmother rides a bike to go places.				
Riding a bike is a fun way to exercise.				
This grandmother has fun with her grandchild.				
They can draw pictures with each other.				
What does a grandmother do? She does a lot of				
things!				
Grandmothers are just grand!				
TOTAL				

Key: **RW**=Running Words   **SC**=Self-Correction   **E**=Errors

© Macmillan/McGraw-Hill

Running Record

Level ___6___

Name _____ Date _____

Text ___Grandmothers___

Retelling Rubric

☐ **4** Accurate information, told in sequence, very detailed.

☐ **3** Accurate information, adequate detail and description.

☐ **2** Limited information, few if any details.

☐ **I** Incorrect information, little or no understanding.

Graphic Organizer: _____

Comprehension Check

1. What are some ways grandmothers exercise?

Student Response: _____

2. What are some ways grandmothers have fun?

Student Response: _____

Reading Level

Error Rate $1 : \dfrac{(RW)}{(E)}$ _____ *

*Use the ratio and refer to the Conversion Table on page 7 to get a **reading accuracy percentage.**

Reading Accuracy Percentage: _____ %

Self-Correction Rate $1 : \dfrac{(E) + (SC)}{(SC)}$

Observed Reading Behaviors

- moves left to right on one line of text ☐
- demonstrates control of one to one matching ☐
- rereads to confirm and search for meaning ☐
- uses intonation and expression ☐
- uses phrasing ☐
- uses picture cues to confirm context and visual cues ☐

At points of difficulty, the student will _____

© Macmillan/McGraw-Hill

Running Record

Level: __8__

Name: _____

Age: _____ RW: __110__

Text: __Show and Tell__

Reading Accuracy Percentage: _____

Circle Reading Level: Independent   Instructional   Frustrational

SC Rate: _____

	E	SC	MSV(E)	MSV(SC)
This is a story that ends with a surprise!				
Mrs. James said, "Hello boys and girls! Today is Show and Tell Day. What do you have to tell?"				
Ray said, "I walked to school today. The bus was late. My dad walked with me."				
"I hit a home run," said Kate. "I helped win the game! It was fun to win."				
"Do you have something to show?" asked Mrs. James. She looked around at all the hands that were up.				
Matt said, "I have a plant for the bunny to eat." Matt showed the boys and girls the plant. Russ sniffed the plant like a bunny.				
Sunny said, "Look at the bunny!" Under the bunny were three baby bunnies!				
TOTAL				

Key: RW=Running Words   **SC**=Self-Correction   **E**=Errors

Running Record

Level __8__

Name _____ Date _____

Text __Show and Tell__ _____

Retelling Rubric

☐ **4** Accurate information, told in sequence, very detailed.

☐ **3** Accurate information, adequate detail and description.

☐ **2** Limited information, few if any details.

☐ **1** Incorrect information, little or no understanding.

Graphic Organizer: _____

Comprehension Check

1. Why did Ray have to walk to school?

Student Response: _____

2. Why did Matt bring a plant?

Student Response: _____

Reading Level

Error Rate $1 : \dfrac{(RW)}{(E)}$ _____ *

*Use the ratio and refer to the Conversion Table on page 7 to get a **reading accuracy percentage.**

Reading Accuracy Percentage: _____ %

Self-Correction Rate $1 : \dfrac{(E) + (SC)}{(SC)}$

Observed Reading Behaviors

- moves left to right on one line of text ☐
- demonstrates control of one to one matching ☐
- rereads to confirm and search for meaning ☐
- uses intonation and expression ☐
- uses phrasing ☐
- uses picture cues to confirm context and visual cues ☐

At points of difficulty, the student will _____

_____

© Macmillan/McGraw-Hill

Running Record

Level: 8

Name: _____ Age: _____ RW: 101

Text: Toads Reading Accuracy Percentage: _____

Circle Reading Level: Independent   Instructional   Frustrational   SC Rate: _____

	E	SC	MSV(E)	MSV(SC)
This book is all about toads.				
Do you know where toads live?				
They live on land but toads also live in water.				
Where do toads lay their eggs?				
They lay their eggs in water. The eggs hatch in water, too.				
This looks like a small fish but it is not.				
It is a baby toad. The name for a baby toad is a tadpole.				
Some toads live in a log.				
All toads have bumps on their skin.				
Toads have to find their food. They eat bugs, flies, and spiders.				
A toad uses its tongue to trap a bug.				
Do you think this toad will trap the worm?				
TOTAL				

Key: RW=Running Words   **SC**=Self-Correction   **E**=Errors

© Macmillan/McGraw-Hill

54 • Running Record • Level 8

Running Record

Level __8__

Name _____ Date _____

Text __Toads__

Retelling Rubric

☐ **4** Accurate information, told in sequence, very detailed.

☐ **3** Accurate information, adequate detail and description.

☐ **2** Limited information, few if any details.

☐ **I** Incorrect information, little or no understanding.

Graphic Organizer: _____

Comprehension Check

1. Where do toads lay their eggs?

Student Response: _____

2. How do toads trap their food?

Student Response: _____

Reading Level

Error Rate $1: \dfrac{(RW)}{(E)}$ *

*Use the ratio and refer to the Conversion Table on page 7 to get a **reading accuracy percentage.**

Reading Accuracy Percentage: _____ %

Self-Correction Rate $1: \dfrac{(E) + (SC)}{(SC)}$

Observed Reading Behaviors

- moves left to right on one line of text   ☐
- demonstrates control of one to one matching   ☐
- rereads to confirm and search for meaning   ☐
- uses intonation and expression   ☐
- uses phrasing   ☐
- uses picture cues to confirm context and visual cues   ☐

At points of difficulty, the student will _____

© Macmillan/McGraw-Hill

Running Record

Level: __10__

Name: _____ Age: _____ RW: __126__

Text: __Max and I_____ Reading Accuracy Percentage: _____

Circle Reading Level: Independent Instructional Frustrational   SC Rate: _____

			E	SC	MSV(E)	MSV(SC)
This is a story about a girl and her dog.						
I can't forget the first time I saw Max. It was Saturday and I was walking along my street.						
I was swinging a stick in the air. Suddenly, I dropped it.						
A dog grabbed the stick before I could get it. He pushed the stick into my hand!						
I let the dog come inside my house. Max sat and lifted his paw. I think he wanted me to shake it!						
Now we are together all the time. I take care of Max. Max takes care of me.						
Max goes to bed when I go to bed. He gets up when I get up.						
In summer, we play together in the yard.						
Max is the best dog in the world. I'm so lucky that Max found me!						
		TOTAL				

Key: RW=Running Words **SC**=Self-Correction **E**=Errors

© Macmillan/McGraw-Hill

Running Record

Level __10__

Name _____ Date _____

Text __Max and I__

Retelling Rubric

- ☐ **4** Accurate information, told in sequence, very detailed.
- ☐ **3** Accurate information, adequate detail and description.
- ☐ **2** Limited information, few if any details.
- ☐ **1** Incorrect information, little or no understanding.

Graphic Organizer: _____

Comprehension Check

1. How did the girl meet Max, the dog?

Student Response: _____

2. What are three things Max and the girl do?

Student Response: _____

Reading Level

Error Rate $1 : \dfrac{(RW)}{(E)}$ *

*Use the ratio and refer to the Conversion Table on page 7 to get a **reading accuracy percentage.**

Reading Accuracy Percentage: _____ %

Self-Correction Rate $1 : \dfrac{(E) + (SC)}{(SC)}$

Observed Reading Behaviors

- moves left to right on one line of text ☐
- demonstrates control of one to one matching ☐
- rereads to confirm and search for meaning ☐
- uses intonation and expression ☐
- uses phrasing ☐
- uses picture cues to confirm context and visual cues ☐

At points of difficulty, the student will _____

_____

© Macmillan/McGraw-Hill

Running Record

Level: __10__

Name: _____ Age: _____ RW: __121__

Text: __Dolls_____ Reading Accuracy Percentage: _____

Circle Reading Level: Independent   Instructional   Frustrational   SC Rate: _____

	E	SC	MSV(E)	MSV(SC)
This is a story about how dolls were made long ago.				
Dolls come in many shapes and sizes. There are boy dolls and girl dolls.				
Children have always liked playing with dolls. Does that surprise you?				
Children have always liked playing with doll houses, too.				
Let's see how today's dolls are like dolls long ago.				
Some dolls were made of paper. You had to cut them up before playing with them.				
Other dolls were made from wax. When wax is hot, it becomes soft. Then it can be shaped into a doll.				
Long ago, children made their own dolls by hand. They made dolls with old socks, rags, and old buttons.				
Now most children can get their dolls at a store. Would you like to make dolls like children did long ago?				
TOTAL				

Key: RW=Running Words   **SC**=Self-Correction   **E**=Errors

© Macmillan/McGraw-Hill

Running Record

Name _____   Date _____

Text __Dolls__ _____

Retelling Rubric

☐ **4** Accurate information, told in sequence, very detailed.

☐ **3** Accurate information, adequate detail and description.

☐ **2** Limited information, few if any details.

☐ **1** Incorrect information, little or no understanding.

Graphic Organizer: _____

Comprehension Check

1. How were dolls from long ago different from dolls today?

Student Response: _____

2. In what ways are they the same?

Student Response: _____

Reading Level

Error Rate $1 : \dfrac{(RW)}{(E)}$ ____ *

*Use the ratio and refer to the Conversion Table on page 7 to get a **reading accuracy percentage.**

Reading Accuracy Percentage: _____ %

Self-Correction Rate $1 : \dfrac{(E) + (SC)}{(SC)}$

Observed Reading Behaviors

- moves left to right on one line of text   ☐
- demonstrates control of one to one matching   ☐
- rereads to confirm and search for meaning   ☐
- uses intonation and expression   ☐
- uses phrasing   ☐
- uses picture cues to confirm context and visual cues   ☐

At points of difficulty, the student will _____

_____

© Macmillan/McGraw-Hill

Running Record

Level: __12__

Name: _____

Age: _____   RW: __137__

Text: __Johnny Appleseed__

Reading Accuracy Percentage: _____

Circle Reading Level: Independent   Instructional   Frustrational

SC Rate: _____

	E	SC	MSV(E)	MSV(SC)
This is a story about a man who planted apple trees.				
Long ago, there were hardly any apple trees. A boy named Johnny loved these trees. One day he climbed up an old apple tree. He sat on a branch and ate an apple.				
Johnny picked out the seeds from the apple. The light, small seeds in his hand gave him an idea. "I'm going to plant these apple seeds," said Johnny.				
Johnny ate many apples. He'd save the seeds, put them in a sack, and plant them. Johnny explained that one day the seeds would grow into apple trees.				
When he got older, Johnny walked far and wide. Now and then he'd stop to plant an apple seed. People all over the country knew Johnny. They gave him the name Johnny Appleseed.				
The apple seeds Johnny planted started to grow.				
In time, apple trees covered the land.				
TOTAL				

Key: **RW**=Running Words   **SC**=Self-Correction   **E**=Errors

© Macmillan/McGraw-Hill

Running Record

Name _____ Date _____

Text __Johnny Appleseed__ _____

Retelling Rubric

☐ **4** Accurate information, told in sequence, very detailed.

☐ **3** Accurate information, adequate detail and description.

☐ **2** Limited information, few if any details.

☐ **1** Incorrect information, little or no understanding.

Graphic Organizer: _____

Comprehension Check

1. What plan did Johnny make up while he was sitting in a tree?

Student Response: _____

2. How did Johnny help people?

Student Response: _____

Reading Level

Error Rate $1 : \dfrac{(RW)}{(E)}$ *

*Use the ratio and refer to the Conversion Table on page 7 to get a **reading accuracy percentage.**

Reading Accuracy Percentage: _____ %

Self-Correction Rate $1 : \dfrac{(E) + (SC)}{(SC)}$

Observed Reading Behaviors

- moves left to right on one line of text ☐
- demonstrates control of one to one matching ☐
- rereads to confirm and search for meaning ☐
- uses intonation and expression ☐
- uses phrasing ☐
- uses picture cues to confirm context and visual cues ☐

At points of difficulty, the student will _____

© Macmillan/McGraw-Hill

Running Record

Level: __12__

Name: _____   Age: _____   RW: __138__

Text: __See Spain!__   Reading Accuracy Percentage: _____

Circle Reading Level: Independent   Instructional   Frustrational   SC Rate: _____

	E	SC	MSV(E)	MSV(SC)
This book is all about Spain.				
Spain is a very special place.				
The country of Spain is across the ocean. Some people travel by plane or boat just to see Spain.				
Spain is very sunny and it's hot most of the time. It hardly rains so most places in Spain are very dry.				
Spain has beautiful beaches with pink sand and blue water. Tall trees called palm trees help shade people from the hot sun.				
Many homes in Spain are made of stones. The homes are often white with roofs painted orange like the sun.				
Most places shut down for lunch in Spain. People go home to eat and often rest. After they rest, people go back to work.				
During the week, children in Spain go to school. For fun, they can go to the beach and swim.				
Would you like to visit Spain?				
TOTAL				

Key: **RW**=Running Words   **SC**=Self-Correction   **E**=Errors

© Macmillan/McGraw-Hill

Running Record

Name _____ Date _____

Text _See Spain!_____

Retelling Rubric

☐ **4** Accurate information, told in sequence, very detailed.

☐ **3** Accurate information, adequate detail and description.

☐ **2** Limited information, few if any details.

☐ **1** Incorrect information, little or no understanding.

Graphic Organizer: _____

Comprehension Check

1. What is special about lunchtime in Spain?

Student Response: _____

2. What do people see when they travel to Spain?

Student Response: _____

Reading Level

Error Rate $1 : \dfrac{(RW)}{(E)}$ *

*Use the ratio and refer to the Conversion Table on page 7 to get a **reading accuracy percentage.**

Reading Accuracy Percentage: _____ %

Self-Correction Rate $1 : \dfrac{(E) + (SC)}{(SC)}$

Observed Reading Behaviors

- moves left to right on one line of text ☐
- demonstrates control of one to one matching ☐
- rereads to confirm and search for meaning ☐
- uses intonation and expression ☐
- uses phrasing ☐
- uses picture cues to confirm context and visual cues ☐

At points of difficulty, the student will _____

_____

© Macmillan/McGraw-Hill

Running Record

Level: **14**

Name: _____   Age: _____   RW: **151**

Text: **Sally and the Lion** _____

Reading Accuracy Percentage: _____

Circle Reading Level: Independent   Instructional   Frustrational   SC Rate: _____

	E	SC	MSV(E)	MSV(SC)
This story is about a girl who met a lion. Or did she?				
Sally did not feel well and was on her bed. She was looking at a large book. It had pictures of lots of animals in it.				
Sally liked the picture of the lion standing in waving grass. As she looked at the picture, the lion seemed to move towards her!				
"Come with me," the lion said. "You will see what my home is like." Sally got onto the lion's back and ran through the grass.				
The land was dry but there were short trees everywhere. From the lion's back, Sally saw many other interesting animals. They waved their tails as the lion ran past.				
The lion had been running a long time. As it got darker, he stopped to rest. Sally did, too.				
When Sally woke up, her mom was standing beside her.				
Sally smiled and said, "I had the strangest dream, Mom. The lion in the book came to life!"				
TOTAL				

Key: **RW**=Running Words   **SC**=Self-Correction   **E**=Errors

© Macmillan/McGraw-Hill

Running Record

Name _____ Date _____

Text <u>Sally and the Lion</u>

_____

Retelling Rubric

☐ **4** Accurate information, told in sequence, very detailed.

☐ **3** Accurate information, adequate detail and description.

☐ **2** Limited information, few if any details.

☐ **1** Incorrect information, little or no understanding.

Graphic Organizer: _____

Comprehension Check

1. What happened to Sally in the story?

Student Response: _____

2. Did Sally really meet the lion? How do you know?

Student Response: _____

Reading Level

Error Rate $1 : \dfrac{(RW)}{(E)}$ *

*Use the ratio and refer to the Conversion Table on page 7 to get a **reading accuracy percentage.**

Reading Accuracy Percentage: _____ %

Self-Correction Rate $1 : \dfrac{(E) + (SC)}{(SC)}$

Observed Reading Behaviors

- moves left to right on one line of text   ☐
- demonstrates control of one to one matching   ☐
- rereads to confirm and search for meaning   ☐
- uses intonation and expression   ☐
- uses phrasing   ☐
- uses picture cues to confirm context and visual cues ☐

At points of difficulty, the student will _____

_____

© Macmillan/McGraw-Hill

Running Record

Level: __14__

Name: _____

Age: _____ RW: __149__

Text: __Teeth__

Reading Accuracy Percentage: _____

Circle Reading Level: Independent   Instructional   Frustrational   SC Rate: _____

	E	SC	MSV(E)	MSV(SC)
This book tells you how to take care of your teeth.				
Teeth grow in our mouths. You can see part of a tooth, but not all of it.				
Without teeth, you couldn't bite, cut, or chew your food. We could only drink or eat mushy food. Teeth come in different shapes and sizes. Baby teeth fall out so that bigger teeth can grow in.				
The crown is the part of the tooth you can see. The crown is very hard and protects your tooth.				
You can't see a tooth's root. It's inside the skin or gum. The root keeps your tooth in place.				
It's important to take care of your teeth. Brushing after each meal is best. Have your teeth checked by a dentist twice a year.				
Don't eat snacks with sugar. Eat fruits and vegetables instead. Also, drink lots of milk. Take care of your teeth now. You'll help your teeth stay healthy for the rest of your life.				
TOTAL				

Key: RW=Running Words   **SC**=Self-Correction   **E**=Errors

© Macmillan/McGraw-Hill

Running Record

Name _____ Date _____

Text __Teeth__ _____

Retelling Rubric

☐ **4** Accurate information, told in sequence, very detailed.

☐ **3** Accurate information, adequate detail and description.

☐ **2** Limited information, few if any details.

☐ **1** Incorrect information, little or no understanding.

Graphic Organizer: _____

Comprehension Check

1. Describe the different parts of a tooth.

Student Response: _____

2. What are two ways you can keep your teeth clean and healthy?

Student Response: _____

Reading Level

Error Rate $1 : \dfrac{(RW)}{(E)}$ *

*Use the ratio and refer to the Conversion Table on page 7 to get a **reading accuracy percentage.**

Reading Accuracy Percentage: _____ %

Self-Correction Rate $1 : \dfrac{(E) + (SC)}{(SC)}$

Observed Reading Behaviors

- moves left to right on one line of text ☐
- demonstrates control of one to one matching ☐
- rereads to confirm and search for meaning ☐
- uses intonation and expression ☐
- uses phrasing ☐
- uses picture cues to confirm context and visual cues ☐

At points of difficulty, the student will _____

_____

© Macmillan/McGraw-Hill

Running Record

Level: 16

Name: _____

Age: _____   RW: 161

Text: Black Crow's Nest

Reading Accuracy Percentage: _____

Circle Reading Level: Independent   Instructional   Frustrational

SC Rate: _____

	E	SC	MSV(E)	MSV(SC)
This is a story about how Black Crow builds her nest.				
All the birds in the forest, except for one, were building their nests.				
Black Crow didn't want to build her nest. So she sat and ate her dinner.				
Black Crow saw Blue Jay in the sky. Black Crow asked why she was carrying sticks and twigs.				
"I'm busy building my nest," answered Blue Jay. "It takes time to build a beautiful nest like mine!"				
Black Crow went to see Duck. When Duck came up for air, her mouth was full of mud. Duck explained that she was making her nest and was too busy to talk.				
Black Crow went to visit Robin but Robin's mouth was full of feathers.				
Robin told Black Crow, "Feathers keep the nest nice and warm."				
It was time for Black Crow to lay her eggs. She needed a nest in a hurry. She pushed together twigs, mud, and feathers and her nest was done.				
Now you know why a black crow's nest is such a mess!				
TOTAL				

Key: RW=Running Words   **SC**=Self-Correction   **E**=Errors

© Macmillan/McGraw-Hill

Running Record

Name _____ Date _____

Text Black Crow's Nest _____

_____

Retelling Rubric

☐ **4** Accurate information, told in sequence, very detailed.

☐ **3** Accurate information, adequate detail and description.

☐ **2** Limited information, few if any details.

☐ **1** Incorrect information, little or no understanding.

Graphic Organizer: _____

Comprehension Check

1. How are Blue Jay's and Robin's nests different?

Student Response: _____

2. Why did Black Crow have to build her nest so quickly?

Student Response: _____

Reading Level

Error Rate $1 : \dfrac{(RW)}{(E)}$ *

*Use the ratio and refer to the Conversion Table on page 7 to get a **reading accuracy percentage.**

Reading Accuracy Percentage: _____ %

Self-Correction Rate $1 : \dfrac{(E) + (SC)}{(SC)}$

Observed Reading Behaviors

- moves left to right on one line of text ☐
- demonstrates control of one to one matching ☐
- rereads to confirm and search for meaning ☐
- uses intonation and expression ☐
- uses phrasing ☐
- uses picture cues to confirm context and visual cues ☐

At points of difficulty, the student will _____

_____

© Macmillan/McGraw-Hill

Running Record

Level: 16

Name: _____ Age: _____ RW: 157

Text: How We Carry Babies

Reading Accuracy Percentage: _____

Circle Reading Level: Independent   Instructional   Frustrational   SC Rate: _____

	E	SC	MSV(E)	MSV(SC)
This book is about the different ways we carry babies.				
How do babies get around?				
Babies can't walk so grown ups have to pick them up and carry them.				
Moms and dads carry babies. Let's take a look at how babies get around.				
Sometimes brothers carry babies. This boy is helping out his parents by carrying his sister.				
This girl wears a special cloth to carry her brother. The cloth wraps around her and the baby.				
This mother is carrying her baby in a sling. The sling makes it easier to hold the baby. The mother and baby can look at each other, too.				
Sometimes people carry their babies in blankets on their backs. A blanket keeps the baby warm and snug. Doesn't the baby look happy?				
This baby is also on her mother's back. The mother's hands are free to carry other things.				
In China, a baby sling is made from red cloth. Red means good luck in China.				
Now you know how babies get around!				
TOTAL				

Key: **RW**=Running Words   **SC**=Self-Correction   **E**=Errors

© Macmillan/McGraw-Hill

Running Record

Level __16__

Name _____ Date _____

Text __How We Carry Babies__

_____

Retelling Rubric

☐ **4** Accurate information, told in sequence, very detailed.

☐ **3** Accurate information, adequate detail and description.

☐ **2** Limited information, few if any details.

☐ **I** Incorrect information, little or no understanding.

Graphic Organizer: _____

Comprehension Check

I. What are two ways babies are carried?

Student Response: _____

2. Why do many Chinese mothers use red slings for babies?

Student Response: _____

Reading Level

Error Rate I: $\dfrac{(RW)}{(E)}$ *

*Use the ratio and refer to the Conversion Table on page 7 to get a **reading accuracy percentage.**

Reading Accuracy Percentage: _____ %

Self-Correction Rate I: $\dfrac{(E) + (SC)}{(SC)}$

Observed Reading Behaviors

• moves left to right on one line of text   ☐

• demonstrates control of one to one matching   ☐

• rereads to confirm and search for meaning   ☐

• uses intonation and expression   ☐

• uses phrasing   ☐

• uses picture cues to confirm context and visual cues   ☐

At points of difficulty, the student will _____

© Macmillan/McGraw-Hill

Running Record

Level: __18__

Name: _____

Age: _____ RW: __209__

Text: __The Tailor's Trick__

Reading Accuracy Percentage: _____

Circle Reading Level: Independent   Instructional   Frustrational

SC Rate: _____

	E	SC	MSV(E)	MSV(SC)
This is a story about a tailor who tricked two giants.				
There once lived a young tailor named Thomas. His wish was to marry the king's daughter, Princess Emma.				
The king posted a sign. He promised that whoever got rid of two very nasty giants could marry Princess Emma. Grim and Glum were the giants' names.				
Thomas snuck up to the giants' cave and heard them shouting. Grim wanted a big fat sheep to eat but Glum was too tired to hunt.				
Thomas ran back to his shop. The two giants had given him an idea!				
Back in his shop, the tailor started sewing. He made the largest sheep costume ever!				
That night as the giants slept, Thomas crept back to the cave. He carefully put the sheep costume on Glum. Then Thomas hid in the bushes and waited until morning.				
When Grim woke up, he saw an enormous sheep asleep. He called to Glum to get the sheep. When sleepy Glum woke up, he ran out of the cave. Grim ran out, too. Grim thought he was chasing the sheep but he was chasing Glum! The two giants kept running and were never seen again. The tailor told the king the good news. The king kept his word. The princess and Thomas were married and lived happily ever after!				
TOTAL				

Key: **RW**=Running Words   **SC**=Self-Correction   **E**=Errors

© Macmillan/McGraw-Hill

Running Record

Level __18__

Name _____ Date _____

Text __The Tailor's Trick__ _____

Retelling Rubric

☐ **4** Accurate information, told in sequence, very detailed.

☐ **3** Accurate information, adequate detail and description.

☐ **2** Limited information, few if any details.

☐ **1** Incorrect information, little or no understanding.

Graphic Organizer: _____

Comprehension Check

1. Why did the tailor want to get rid of the giants?

Student Response: _____

2. How did the tailor trick the giants?

Student Response: _____

Reading Level

Error Rate $1 : \dfrac{(RW)}{(E)}$ _____ *

*Use the ratio and refer to the Conversion Table on page 7 to get a **reading accuracy percentage.**

Reading Accuracy Percentage: _____ %

Self-Correction Rate $1 : \dfrac{(E) + (SC)}{(SC)}$

Observed Reading Behaviors

- moves left to right on one line of text ☐
- demonstrates control of one to one matching ☐
- rereads to confirm and search for meaning ☐
- uses intonation and expression ☐
- uses phrasing ☐
- uses picture cues to confirm context and visual cues ☐

At points of difficulty, the student will _____

_____

© Macmillan/McGraw-Hill

Running Record

Level: _____18_____

Name: _____   Age: _____   RW: _____199_____

Text: ___Water_____   Reading Accuracy Percentage: _____

Circle Reading Level: Independent   Instructional   Frustrational   SC Rate: _____

	E	SC	MSV(E)	MSV(SC)
This book is all about water.				
Everyone on Earth uses water. People and plants need water to live. How do you use water?				
Rain, steam, and ice are all forms of water. Water can change from one form to another. Water can be a solid, liquid, or gas.				
When water gets very cold, it freezes and turns to ice. Ice is the solid form of water. There are places in the world where there is ice all year round.				
Rain is liquid water. On rainy days, you can see water fall in drops from the sky. The water is coming from the clouds.				
Water can turn into gas called water vapor. Water vapor is made up of tiny drops of water. It's not always easy to see water vapor. Steam rising from boiling water is an example of water vapor.				
All of the water on Earth is part of the water cycle. The water cycle begins when the sun warms the water in oceans and rivers. The sun's heat makes the water change into water vapor. Then the water vapor rises into the sky. When the water droplets get big and stick together, clouds form. Finally, the water drops fall back to Earth as rain.				
TOTAL				

Key: RW=Running Words   **SC**=Self-Correction   **E**=Errors

© Macmillan/McGraw-Hill

Running Record

Name _____ Date _____

Text __Water__ _____

Retelling Rubric

☐ **4** Accurate information, told in sequence, very detailed.

☐ **3** Accurate information, adequate detail and description.

☐ **2** Limited information, few if any details.

☐ **I** Incorrect information, little or no understanding.

Graphic Organizer: _____

Comprehension Check

1. Give an example of water as a solid, a liquid, and a gas.

Student Response: _____

2. What causes water to change into vapor?

Student Response: _____

Reading Level

Error Rate $1 : \dfrac{(RW)}{(E)}$ *

*Use the ratio and refer to the Conversion Table on page 7 to get a **reading accuracy percentage.**

Reading Accuracy Percentage: _____ %

Self-Correction Rate $1 : \dfrac{(E) + (SC)}{(SC)}$

Observed Reading Behaviors

- moves left to right on one line of text   ☐
- demonstrates control of one to one matching   ☐
- rereads to confirm and search for meaning   ☐
- uses intonation and expression   ☐
- uses phrasing   ☐
- uses picture cues to confirm context and visual cues   ☐

At points of difficulty, the student will _____

_____

© Macmillan/McGraw-Hill

Running Record

Level: 20

Name: _____   Age: _____   RW: 225

Text: Where Is Uncle Joe's Hat?

Reading Accuracy Percentage: _____

Circle Reading Level: Independent   Instructional   Frustrational   SC Rate: _____

	E	SC	MSV(E)	MSV(SC)
This is a story about a lost hat.				
My Uncle Joe has a hat he loves so much that he never takes it off until he goes to bed. It's the last thing he does each night. The first thing he does each morning is put the hat back on his head!				
One day, when Uncle Joe woke up, he couldn't find his hat. After he checked his bedroom, he looked in all the closets. He even looked in the oven but the hat was nowhere to be found.				
"Someone has stolen my hat! Has anyone seen it?" he shouted.				
Uncle Joe's cat, Whiskers, woke up and started meowing.				
"Be quiet, Whiskers! Unless you can tell me where my hat is, keep quiet!"				
Whiskers' feelings were hurt. So she went back to sleep.				
Poor Uncle Joe! He lost his favorite hat so he can't function at all. He doesn't know what to do.				
Worried, Uncle Joe got ready for work. Suddenly, he heard Whiskers meowing and meowing. She wasn't on her seat anymore.				
"Did I forget to feed my kitty?" wondered Uncle Joe. "I believe I fed Whiskers. I wonder what the matter could be."				
So Uncle Joe went outside to find the cat and found his hat, too. He also found five little kittens inside the hat. Uncle Joe's hat was a nice, cozy home for Whiskers and her five newborn kittens!				
TOTAL				

Key: RW=Running Words   **SC**=Self-Correction   **E**=Errors

© Macmillan/McGraw-Hill

Running Record

Level __20__

Name _____ Date _____

Text _Where Is Uncle Joe's Hat?_

Retelling Rubric

☐ **4** Accurate information, told in sequence, very detailed.

☐ **3** Accurate information, adequate detail and description.

☐ **2** Limited information, few if any details.

☐ **1** Incorrect information, little or no understanding.

Graphic Organizer: _____

Comprehension Check

1. Why does Uncle Joe always wear his hat?

Student Response: _____

2. Why couldn't Uncle Joe find his hat?

Student Response: _____

Reading Level

Error Rate $1 : \dfrac{(RW)}{(E)}$ *

*Use the ratio and refer to the Conversion Table on page 7 to get a **reading accuracy percentage.**

Reading Accuracy Percentage: _____ %

Self-Correction Rate $1 : \dfrac{(E) + (SC)}{(SC)}$

Observed Reading Behaviors

- moves left to right on one line of text ☐
- demonstrates control of one to one matching ☐
- rereads to confirm and search for meaning ☐
- uses intonation and expression ☐
- uses phrasing ☐
- uses picture cues to confirm context and visual cues ☐

At points of difficulty, the student will _____

_____

© Macmillan/McGraw-Hill

Running Record

Level: 20

Name: _____   Age: _____   RW: 219

Text: Watch It Grow!   Reading Accuracy Percentage: _____

Circle Reading Level: Independent   Instructional   Frustrational   SC Rate: _____

	E	SC	MSV(E)	MSV(SC)
This book will tell you how plants can grow in water.				
Did you know that some plants can grow in water? Bean plants can.				
Place a bean plant in a jar of water and it will sprout. Use a pencil and paper to record what happens.				
The bean seed uses the water in the jar. This helps it grow. Then the seed will crack open. Next you'll observe something that looks like hair growing out of the seed. These are the plant's roots.				
How does a seed get the nutrients it needs? The seed gets its food and water through the roots. More roots will grow and the stem will start to grow too.				
You'll also notice a small green shoot. Then a seedling grows and tiny leaves form. As the seedling grows, the stem will get thicker and fatter.				
Now place the plant on a sunny window sill. This plant needs light from the sun to help it grow. If it doesn't get enough light, the plant will soon die. Try this! Turn the plant away from the window. The plant will bend to face the light. This proves how much this plant needs sun.				
Next, you'll observe that the leaves grow bigger and the beans start to grow too. Very soon, you'll have a tall bean plant! Use the beans from this plant to grow new bean plants.				
TOTAL				

Key: RW=Running Words   **SC**=Self-Correction   **E**=Errors

© Macmillan/McGraw-Hill

Running Record

Level _20_

Name _____ Date _____

Text _Watch It Grow!_ _____

Retelling Rubric

☐ **4** Accurate information, told in sequence, very detailed.

☐ **3** Accurate information, adequate detail and description.

☐ **2** Limited information, few if any details.

☐ **I** Incorrect information, little or no understanding.

Graphic Organizer: _____

Comprehension Check

I. What are the tiny hairs that first come out of the seed?

Student Response: _____

2. What should you do after you see the stem grow out of the seed?

Student Response: _____

Reading Level

Error Rate $1: \dfrac{(RW)}{(E)}$ *

*Use the ratio and refer to the Conversion Table on page 7 to get a **reading accuracy percentage.**

Reading Accuracy Percentage: _____ %

Self-Correction Rate $1: \dfrac{(E) + (SC)}{(SC)}$

Observed Reading Behaviors

- moves left to right on one line of text ☐
- demonstrates control of one to one matching ☐
- rereads to confirm and search for meaning ☐
- uses intonation and expression ☐
- uses phrasing ☐
- uses picture cues to confirm context and visual cues ☐

At points of difficulty, the student will _____

_____

© Macmillan/McGraw-Hill

Running Record

Level: __24__

Name: _____   Age: _____   RW: __240__

Text: __The Secret_____

Reading Accuracy Percentage: _____

Circle Reading Level: **Independent**   Instructional   Frustrational   SC Rate: _____

	E	SC	MSV(E)	MSV(SC)
This story is about two boys and their secret invention.				
Sid and Adam worked secretly for six months on a big invention. Adam did the writing and Sid did the drawings. They hoped to become famous one day.				
Sid could stay out longer than Adam. Adam's parents said to be home by eight. Sid's dad said nine was okay. So Sid often worked alone.				
After Adam went home, he got messages from Sid. Bailey, Sid's dog, was the messenger. Sid tucked the messages in Bailey's leather collar.				
Sometimes the messages were about new ideas that Sid had. Other times, the messages were about what time to meet the next day.				
One day Sid and Adam heard noises coming from their secret planning room in the backyard shed. They raced toward the shed. Who was making the noise? Who had found out about the secret?				
Sid's face turned red. He was angry. "Adam, did you tell anyone about our invention?" he asked.				
Adam was annoyed and answered, "How could you ask me that? I would never tell anyone!"				
The boys listened outside the shed door. Could there be a thief in there? Adam and Sid knew they had to be brave. As Sid gently pulled the door, Adam was ready with a stick. The old door swung open.				
There in the shed was Bailey, Sid's dog, munching on crackers.				
"I can't believe we left the snacks in here!" said Adam.				
Sid answered, "I'm just glad that our secret invention is safe!"				
TOTAL				

Key: RW=Running Words **SC**=Self-Correction **E**=Errors

© Macmillan/McGraw-Hill

Running Record

Name _____ Date _____

Text __The Secret__ _____

Retelling Rubric

☐ **4** Accurate information, told in sequence, very detailed.

☐ **3** Accurate information, adequate detail and description.

☐ **2** Limited information, few if any details.

☐ **I** Incorrect information, little or no understanding.

Graphic Organizer: _____

Comprehension Check

1. Why did Sid sometimes have to work on his own?

Student Response: _____

2. Why did the boys think someone found out their secret?

Student Response: _____

Reading Level

Error Rate $1 : \dfrac{(RW)}{(E)}$ *

*Use the ratio and refer to the Conversion Table on page 7 to get a **reading accuracy percentage.**

Reading Accuracy Percentage: _____ %

Self-Correction Rate $1 : \dfrac{(E) + (SC)}{(SC)}$

Observed Reading Behaviors

- moves left to right on one line of text ☐
- demonstrates control of one to one matching ☐
- rereads to confirm and search for meaning ☐
- uses intonation and expression ☐
- uses phrasing ☐
- uses picture cues to confirm context and visual cues ☐

At points of difficulty, the student will _____

_____

© Macmillan/McGraw-Hill

Running Record

Level: 24

Name: _____ Age: _____ RW: 234

Text: Ostriches _____

Reading Accuracy Percentage: _____

Circle Reading Level: **Independent**   Instructional   Frustrational

SC Rate: _____

	E	SC	MSV(E)	MSV(SC)
This book will tell you all about ostriches.				
Ostriches are the largest birds in the world. With their small heads and long necks, the nickname for an ostrich is "camel sparrow".				
These birds do not fly but can run very fast on their long legs. When fully grown, ostriches stand at least six feet tall.				
Ostriches have enormous feet. There are two toes on each foot. The inner toe is much larger and holds most of the ostrich's weight.				
When it's time for laying eggs, female ostriches share one large nest. The nest is a hole in the ground. It holds 50 or 60 eggs at one time.				
Each ostrich egg weighs over three pounds and has a hard shell. Would you believe that a man can stand on ostrich eggs and not crack them?				
It takes about six weeks for ostrich eggs to hatch. Then the fathers take care of the babies. Most ostriches live about 50 years.				
Ostrich feathers aren't stiff like other birds' feathers. Ostrich feathers are very soft to help keep ostriches warm in cold weather. Mother ostriches also use their wings to shade their chicks from the hot sun.				
Ostriches are originally from Africa where they travel in groups called herds. A herd can be as small as 5 to as large as 50 ostriches.				
With good eyesight and hearing, ostriches are always on the alert. They can spy a lion or other enemy from far away.				
TOTAL				

Key: RW=Running Words   **SC**=Self-Correction   **E**=Errors

© Macmillan/McGraw-Hill

Running Record

Name _____ Date _____

Text __Ostriches_____

Retelling Rubric

☐ **4** Accurate information, told in sequence, very detailed.

☐ **3** Accurate information, adequate detail and description.

☐ **2** Limited information, few if any details.

☐ **1** Incorrect information, little or no understanding.

Graphic Organizer: _____

Comprehension Check

1. How are ostrich nests different from other birds' nests?

Student Response: _____

2. What are two things you learned about ostriches?

Student Response: _____

Reading Level

Error Rate $1 : \dfrac{(RW)}{(E)}$ _____ *

*Use the ratio and refer to the Conversion Table on page 7 to get a **reading accuracy percentage.**

Reading Accuracy Percentage: _____ %

Self-Correction Rate $1 : \dfrac{(E) + (SC)}{(SC)}$ _____

Observed Reading Behaviors

- moves left to right on one line of text   ☐
- demonstrates control of one to one matching   ☐
- rereads to confirm and search for meaning   ☐
- uses intonation and expression   ☐
- uses phrasing   ☐
- uses picture cues to confirm context and visual cues   ☐

At points of difficulty, the student will _____

_____

© Macmillan/McGraw-Hill

Running Record

Level: __28__

Name: _____   Age: _____   RW: __262__

Text: E-mail Joy _____   Reading Accuracy Percentage: _____

Circle Reading Level: **Independent**   Instructional   Frustrational   SC Rate: _____

	E	SC	MSV(E)	MSV(SC)
This is a story about a girl and her new computer.				
For months Tina wanted a computer of her very own. Finally, Tina had saved some money and her parents helped her to buy a new computer. Tina couldn't wait to e-mail her friends!				
When the computer was finally connected, Tina wrote to her friend Fay, then to Jennifer. Tina wrote short messages since she had seen both of her friends that day.				
Tina kept checking but no e-mails came in from Fay or from Jennifer. When Tina went to sleep that night, she still hadn't heard from either friend.				
Early the next morning, Tina checked her e-mail again. Jennifer had answered! Tina eagerly opened up the e-mail message. Jennifer had written back with only one word "Okay". Tina was very disappointed.				
What was the point in saving for the computer when her friends weren't going to send back messages?				
Tina came up with a new plan. She asked her mother for her relatives' e-mail addresses. Her mom was very puzzled, but gave Tina as many addresses as she had.				
Tina went straight to work. She took a while to find the right words to express just what she wanted to say. She did a spell check. Then she copied and pasted what she wrote into the e-mails. She pressed the SEND button and hoped she'd hear from everyone.				
The next morning, Tina opened her e-mail and saw a picture. It was a picture of Uncle Dan's family with their new dog Freddy!				
Tina thought, "I'm going to get to know my entire family! This is the best thing I've ever done!"				
TOTAL				

Key: RW=Running Words   **SC**=Self-Correction   **E**=Errors

© Macmillan/McGraw-Hill

Running Record

Name _____ Date _____

Text E-mail Joy

Retelling Rubric

☐ **4** Accurate information, told in sequence, very detailed.

☐ **3** Accurate information, adequate detail and description.

☐ **2** Limited information, few if any details.

☐ **I** Incorrect information, little or no understanding.

Graphic Organizer: _____

Comprehension Check

1. Why was Tina excited about her new computer?

Student Response: _____

2. Why did Uncle Dan send a photo to Tina?

Student Response: _____

Reading Level

Error Rate $1 : \dfrac{(RW)}{(E)}$ _____ *

*Use the ratio and refer to the Conversion Table on page 7 to get a **reading accuracy percentage.**

Reading Accuracy Percentage: _____ %

Self-Correction Rate $1 : \dfrac{(E) + (SC)}{(SC)}$ _____

Observed Reading Behaviors

- moves left to right on one line of text ☐
- demonstrates control of one to one matching ☐
- rereads to confirm and search for meaning ☐
- uses intonation and expression ☐
- uses phrasing ☐
- uses picture cues to confirm context and visual cues ☐

At points of difficulty, the student will _____

_____

© Macmillan/McGraw-Hill

Running Record

Level: __28__

Name: _____   Age: _____   RW: __257__

Text: __Caterpillars_____

Reading Accuracy Percentage: _____

Circle Reading Level: **Independent**   Instructional   Frustrational   SC Rate: _____

	E	SC	MSV(E)	MSV(SC)
This book will tell you all about caterpillars.				
What is a baby moth or butterfly called? If you guessed caterpillar, you're right! To look at a caterpillar, you'd never dream that it could ever fly. How does a creeping insect change into a flying insect?				
A caterpillar begins its life in an egg. The adult insect lays its eggs on the leaf of a plant. When the egg hatches, a tiny caterpillar comes out and starts to eat the plant's leaves. As it grows, the hungry caterpillar keeps eating leaves.				
A caterpillar will have to start life on its own. It needs to be strong enough to handle the change that is about to happen. The caterpillar will build a cocoon and transform into a butterfly.				
How do caterpillars protect themselves? Some caterpillars have brightly colored stripes, while others have spiky, long hair. Bright colors warn other animals that this caterpillar doesn't taste very good. Spiky long hairs will sting a bird that tries to eat it.				
There's a reason why a caterpillar has a funny way of walking. All caterpillars have three pairs of real legs and up to five pairs of false legs. The real legs have knees but the false legs have little hooks on them. The little hooks help the caterpillar grip things.				
When a caterpillar has grown bigger, it starts to make silk. It weaves a silk cocoon around itself. The air makes the silk get hard. The hard silk protects the caterpillar as it changes into a butterfly or moth. Soon the caterpillar will look just like its parents!				
TOTAL				

Key: RW=Running Words   **SC**=Self-Correction   **E**=Errors

© Macmillan/McGraw-Hill

Running Record

Name _____ Date _____

Text __Caterpillars__

Retelling Rubric

☐ **4** Accurate information, told in sequence, very detailed.

☐ **3** Accurate information, adequate detail and description.

☐ **2** Limited information, few if any details.

☐ **1** Incorrect information, little or no understanding.

Graphic Organizer: _____

Comprehension Check

1. What makes caterpillars walk in a funny way?

Student Response: _____

2. What happens to a caterpillar when it is in its cocoon?

Student Response: _____

Reading Level

Error Rate $1 : \dfrac{(RW)}{(E)}$ _____ *

*Use the ratio and refer to the Conversion Table on page 7 to get a **reading accuracy percentage.**

Reading Accuracy Percentage: _____ %

Self-Correction Rate $1 : \dfrac{(E) + (SC)}{(SC)}$

Observed Reading Behaviors

- moves left to right on one line of text ☐
- demonstrates control of one to one matching ☐
- rereads to confirm and search for meaning ☐
- uses intonation and expression ☐
- uses phrasing ☐
- uses picture cues to confirm context and visual cues ☐

At points of difficulty, the student will _____

_____

© Macmillan/McGraw-Hill

Running Record

Level: __30__

Name: _____

Age: _____

RW: __245__

Text: __Peter and the Dragon__

Reading Accuracy Percentage: _____

Circle Reading Level: **Independent**   **Instructional**   **Frustrational**

SC Rate: _____

	E	SC	MSV(E)	MSV(SC)
This is a story about a boy who saved his town from a dragon.				

A long time ago, in a land far away, there lived a dragon. He frightened all the people who lived in the town. Every time he was hungry, someone would disappear! The king offered a reward of one hundred bags of gold to anybody brave enough to make the dragon stop snacking on people.

Peter was the son of the best baker in the land. His job was to take cakes to the king's palace. Peter spent many hours wishing he was brave enough to face the dragon. One day, when he was planning what he could do with one hundred bags of gold, he got lost on his way to the palace. Without warning, he felt the ground tremble beneath him and he heard the roar of a terrible beast. **131 words**

There was the dragon showing his large teeth. Peter did not feel very brave. But he gathered up his courage and said, "Please don't eat me. My father is the best pastry cook in the whole land!" The dragon answered with a roar. "I can bring you cakes for the rest of your life!" cried Peter.

The dragon stopped in the middle of a roar. "Can you bring me those little cakes with pink icing?" he asked.

The next day, Peter returned with his father's best cakes. From then on the dragon lost his taste for people and was happy to eat cakes every day. Peter was happy with one hundred bags of gold!

	TOTAL			

Key: RW=Running Words   **SC**=Self-Correction   **E**=Errors

© Macmillan/McGraw-Hill

Running Record

Level <u>30</u>

Name _____   Date _____

Text <u>Peter and the Dragon</u> _____

Retelling Rubric

☐ **4** Accurate information, told in sequence, very detailed.

☐ **3** Accurate information, adequate detail and description.

☐ **2** Limited information, few if any details.

☐ **I** Incorrect information, little or no understanding.

Graphic Organizer: _____

Comprehension Check

1. What was Peter's problem in this story?

Student Response: _____

2. How did Peter solve his problem?

Student Response: _____

Reading Level

Error Rate $1 : \dfrac{(RW)}{(E)}$ _____ *

*Use the ratio and refer to the Conversion Table on page 7 to get a **reading accuracy percentage.**

Reading Accuracy Percentage: _____ %

Self-Correction Rate $1 : \dfrac{(E) + (SC)}{(SC)}$

Observed Reading Behaviors

- moves left to right on one line of text   ☐
- demonstrates control of one to one matching   ☐
- rereads to confirm and search for meaning   ☐
- uses intonation and expression   ☐
- uses phrasing   ☐
- uses picture cues to confirm context and visual cues   ☐

At points of difficulty, the student will _____

Level 30 • Running Record • **89**

Running Record

Level: 30

Name: _____

Age: _____   RW: 240

Text: __Glassblowing_____

Reading Accuracy Percentage: _____

Circle Reading Level: Independent   Instructional   Frustrational   SC Rate: _____

	E	SC	MSV(E)	MSV(SC)
This is a passage about how glass is made.				
Everywhere in the world people make lovely objects out of glass. Glass can be clear or colored, thick or thin. It can be made by machine or by hand.				
Today you find glass used in many places and for many objects. Glass is used to make more than 50,000 products! You find glass in your home, in your school, and in your car. Glass is used for windows and mirrors and televisions. It is made into dishes, bowls, and cups. It is crafted into beautiful jewelry.				
Glass is made from sand which is heated until it melts and becomes a clear liquid. Then a glassblower dips a tube called a blowpipe into this liquid glass so that a bead forms on the end. Then he blows steadily into the tube until the bead becomes a hollow balloon. **137 words**				
Now the glassblower can bend and shape the soft glass balloon to create objects. He can roll and stretch the glass. He puts it on a cold, steel bench called an anvil. Then he uses scissors and tweezers to make the shape he wants to make. As the glass cools it is wiped with a wet leather cloth. Finally, it is left standing to become cold, smooth, and hard.				
How long does glass last? Glass objects can last for a very long time. People who study objects from the past often find glass cups and jewelry that were made hundreds of years ago.				
TOTAL				

© Macmillan/McGraw-Hill

Key: RW=Running Words   **SC**=Self-Correction   **E**=Errors

Running Record

Name _____ Date _____

Text _Glassblowing_

Retelling Rubric

☐ **4** Accurate information, told in sequence, very detailed.

☐ **3** Accurate information, adequate detail and description.

☐ **2** Limited information, few if any details.

☐ **1** Incorrect information, little or no understanding.

Graphic Organizer: _____

Comprehension Check

1. What step does a glassblower take to make glass?

Student Response: _____

2. How did glassblowers probably get their name?

Student Response: _____

Reading Level

Error Rate $1: \dfrac{(RW)}{(E)}$ ____ *

*Use the ratio and refer to the Conversion Table on page 7 to get a **reading accuracy percentage.**

Reading Accuracy Percentage: _____ %

Self-Correction Rate $1: \dfrac{(E) + (SC)}{(SC)}$

Observed Reading Behaviors

- moves left to right on one line of text ☐
- demonstrates control of one to one matching ☐
- rereads to confirm and search for meaning ☐
- uses intonation and expression ☐
- uses phrasing ☐
- uses picture cues to confirm context and visual cues ☐

At points of difficulty, the student will _____
_____

© Macmillan/McGraw-Hill

Running Record

Level: 34

Name: _____   Age: _____   RW: 221

Text: Night Light

Reading Accuracy Percentage: _____

Circle Reading Level: Independent   Instructional   Frustrational   SC Rate: _____

	E	SC	MSV(E)	MSV(SC)
This is a story about a boy who saw a strange light outside his window.				
Max woke up suddenly. What was that sound? He kept perfectly still and listened, but he could not hear anything else. Then he noticed a beam of light move slowly across his bedroom floor, as if a car with its headlights on was passing the window. Only the light was green. Then the beam swept back, from the opposite direction. How could it be car headlights? Max lived in an apartment and his room was on the eighteenth floor.				
Max leapt out of bed and ran to the window to look out. Floating in the air was an oval-shaped, silver spaceship with green lights glowing from its surface. At one end was a headlight shining towards his window. **118 words**				
As he stared without moving, Max thought he could see the shape of a small creature guiding the light toward him. The creature had large round pale eyes and when Max looked at him, their eyes met.				
For a long, quiet moment the two stared at each other. Then suddenly the light went out and Max found himself looking out over the familiar view of the city. Lights twinkled below and the sound of late night traffic rose to his ears.				
No spaceship, no light, no little person. But as Max climbed slowly back into his bed, he knew what he had seen.				
TOTAL				

Key: RW=Running Words   **SC**=Self-Correction   **E**=Errors

© Macmillan/McGraw-Hill

Running Record

Name _____ Date _____

Text __Night Light__

Retelling Rubric

☐ **4** Accurate information, told in sequence, very detailed.

☐ **3** Accurate information, adequate detail and description.

☐ **2** Limited information, few if any details.

☐ **1** Incorrect information, little or no understanding.

Graphic Organizer: _____

Comprehension Check

1. What caused Max to wake up?

Student Response: _____

2. Do you think what Max saw could be real? Why?

Student Response: _____

Reading Level

Error Rate $1: \dfrac{(RW)}{(E)}$ *

*Use the ratio and refer to the Conversion Table on page 7 to get a **reading accuracy percentage.**

Reading Accuracy Percentage: _____ %

Self-Correction Rate $1: \dfrac{(E) + (SC)}{(SC)}$

Observed Reading Behaviors

- moves left to right on one line of text   ☐
- demonstrates control of one to one matching   ☐
- rereads to confirm and search for meaning   ☐
- uses intonation and expression   ☐
- uses phrasing   ☐
- uses picture cues to confirm context and visual cues   ☐

At points of difficulty, the student will _____

© Macmillan/McGraw-Hill

Running Record

Level: 34

Name: _____   Age: _____   RW: 247

Text: Staying Fit _____   Reading Accuracy Percentage: _____

Circle Reading Level: **Independent**   Instructional   Frustrational   SC Rate: _____

	E	SC	MSV(E)	MSV(SC)

This is a passage about staying fit.

Long ago, keeping fit was not a problem for most people. They walked or rode every day as part of their work. Some people had jobs digging, pushing, lifting, or carrying heavy things. This hard work helped to keep people fit. But then times changed. Today fewer people have hard physical jobs. They drive to work in cars or travel on buses, subways, or trains. Many sit at a table or a desk to do their work and do not have an opportunity to walk or run much. As daily life no longer keeps them fit, lots of people turn to sports instead. **103 words**

There are many sports to choose from if you want to keep fit. But when people play a sport they often look for more than just physical fitness. They choose a sport they can play with friends or one that they really enjoy.

Some sports, like soccer, are played with a team that competes with other teams. Playing in a team helps players improve their game. Some teams are made up of five or nine players, but others, like tennis or golf, have one to three players on a team. People who choose these kinds of sports have to practice on their own to get better.

There are still other sports, like swimming, running, skating, and yoga, that people can do alone. Some people enjoy working out in a gym by themselves or with a friend. How would you choose to stay physically fit?

| **TOTAL** | | | | |

Key: RW=Running Words   **SC**=Self-Correction   **E**=Errors

© Macmillan/McGraw-Hill

Name _____ Date _____

Text __Staying Fit__ _____

Retelling Rubric

☐ **4** Accurate information, told in sequence, very detailed.

☐ **3** Accurate information, adequate detail and description.

☐ **2** Limited information, few if any details.

☐ **1** Incorrect information, little or no understanding.

Graphic Organizer: _____

Comprehension Check

1. How are jobs different today than they were in the past?

Student Response: _____

2. What are two ways people can stay fit?

Student Response: _____

Reading Level

Error Rate $1 : \dfrac{(RW)}{(E)}$ _____ *

*Use the ratio and refer to the Conversion Table on page 7 to get a **reading accuracy percentage.**

Reading Accuracy Percentage: _____ %

Self-Correction Rate $1 : \dfrac{(E) + (SC)}{(SC)}$

Observed Reading Behaviors

- moves left to right on one line of text   ☐
- demonstrates control of one to one matching   ☐
- rereads to confirm and search for meaning   ☐
- uses intonation and expression   ☐
- uses phrasing   ☐
- uses picture cues to confirm context and visual cues   ☐

At points of difficulty, the student will _____

© Macmillan/McGraw-Hill

Running Record

Level: __38__

Name: _____   Age: _____   RW: __239__

Text: __The Old Barn__

Reading Accuracy Percentage: _____

Circle Reading Level: Independent   Instructional   Frustrational   SC Rate: _____

		E	SC	MSV(E)	MSV(SC)
This is a story about a girl who liked to hide in an old barn. Nobody ever used the deserted barn in the corner of the open field. In fact, since it seemed so old and broken down, no one even went near it. But it was where Sonia liked to go whenever she felt angry and confused. When she was troubled or unhappy she wanted to be alone and the barn was the best place she knew for being alone. Sonia went through the big door into the coolness of the barn. Once inside, she felt calm and safe. It was totally silent in the dark building; nobody shouted or yelled, and no little brothers whined or teased. Sonia climbed up the steep ladder to the hayloft. As soon as she reached the top she started to feel better. In a corner of the hayloft she had hidden some books and a container filled with cookies. She settled down for a long, peaceful read. **150 words** After a while, Sonia grew calm. She was surprised to realize that she felt lonely for the company of her noisy family. Carefully, she put the lid back on the cookies, and marked her place in her book. Then she left the barn and ran home. Her mom looked up as she walked in. "Hi Mom," said Sonia. "Sorry I gave you such a hard time before. I guess that I was feeling uncomfortable." Mom moved over to make room for Sonia on the couch and said, "Let's talk."					
TOTAL					

Key: RW=Running Words   **SC**=Self-Correction   **E**=Errors

© Macmillan/McGraw-Hill

Running Record

Name _____ Date _____

Text __The Old Barn_____

_____

Retelling Rubric

☐ **4** Accurate information, told in sequence, very detailed.

☐ **3** Accurate information, adequate detail and description.

☐ **2** Limited information, few if any details.

☐ **1** Incorrect information, little or no understanding.

Graphic Organizer: _____

Comprehension Check

1. What made Sonia go to the old barn?

Student Response: _____

2. What do you think Sonia and her mother talked about back home?

Student Response: _____

Reading Level

Error Rate $1 : \dfrac{(RW)}{(E)}$ _____ *

*Use the ratio and refer to the Conversion Table on page 7 to get a **reading accuracy percentage.**

Reading Accuracy Percentage: _____ %

Self-Correction Rate $1 : \dfrac{(E) + (SC)}{(SC)}$ _____

Observed Reading Behaviors

- moves left to right on one line of text ☐
- demonstrates control of one to one matching ☐
- rereads to confirm and search for meaning ☐
- uses intonation and expression ☐
- uses phrasing ☐
- uses picture cues to confirm context and visual cues ☐

At points of difficulty, the student will _____

_____

© Macmillan/McGraw-Hill

Running Record

Level: 38

Name: _____

Age: _____   RW: 221

Text: Keeping It Under Control

Reading Accuracy Percentage: _____

Circle Reading Level: **Independent**   Instructional   Frustrational   SC Rate: _____

	E	SC	MSV(E)	MSV(SC)
This is a passage about finding ways to control feelings of anger.				

We all experience different feelings every day. Some feelings are very enjoyable, like happiness and excitement. Other feelings are not so wonderful. Feeling let down or sad are feelings that are not easy to deal with. Feeling alone can be hard. Probably the most difficult feeling to face is the feeling of anger.

We get angry when we see someone else being hurt or when things happen that do not seem fair or just. Sometimes not getting something we have worked hard for can make us angry. When these things happen, anger can build up inside. This anger stops us from thinking clearly or knowing the right way to act. **110 words**

When you feel this way, it is a good idea to try to tell someone. At first you may not be able to explain how you feel very well. You might not find the right words right away. But you should try. Remember to speak clearly and calmly, and not to shout.

Once someone else knows how you feel, and starts to listen, it gets easier to explain why you feel angry. Using words to express how you feel may also help you know what makes you angry. That will help you do something about the situation. You can start to work out the best way to deal with the anger.

	TOTAL			

Key: RW=Running Words   **SC**=Self-Correction   **E**=Errors

© Macmillan/McGraw-Hill

Running Record

Level <u>38</u>

Name _____ Date _____

Text <u>Keeping It Under Control</u> _____

Retelling Rubric

☐ **4** Accurate information, told in sequence, very detailed.

☐ **3** Accurate information, adequate detail and description.

☐ **2** Limited information, few if any details.

☐ **1** Incorrect information, little or no understanding.

Graphic Organizer: _____

Comprehension Check

1. What are some events that can cause anger?

Student Response: _____

2. What steps can you take when you feel angry?

Student Response: _____

Reading Level

Error Rate $1 : \dfrac{(RW)}{(E)}$ _____ *

*Use the ratio and refer to the Conversion Table on page 7 to get a **reading accuracy percentage.**

Reading Accuracy Percentage: _____ %

Self-Correction Rate $1 : \dfrac{(E) + (SC)}{(SC)}$ _____

Observed Reading Behaviors

- moves left to right on one line of text ☐
- demonstrates control of one to one matching ☐
- rereads to confirm and search for meaning ☐
- uses intonation and expression ☐
- uses phrasing ☐
- uses picture cues to confirm context and visual cues ☐

At points of difficulty, the student will _____
_____

© Macmillan/McGraw-Hill

Running Record

Level: __40__

Name: _____

Age: _____   RW: __252__

Text: __Lucy and Tom_____

Reading Accuracy Percentage: _____

Circle Reading Level: **Independent**   Instructional   Frustrational   SC Rate: _____

	E	SC	MSV(E)	MSV(SC)
This is a story about twins who are very different. Most twins have a lot in common. After all, they grow up in the same house and have the same parents and do many things together. But there are some twins who are different in almost every way. Lucy Layman cares more about sports than anything else. She is an athlete who always wants to be outside playing some sport. She wins every running race she enters and sets records for high jumps and other track events. She can hit more balls on the tennis court than anyone else in her town. Most of all, Lucy loves to play soccer. She practices the game whenever she has a chance and she is an unbeatable force on the soccer field. **119 words** Tom Layman is tall and thin and could be good at sports, but he is just not interested. He would rather read or work on his computer. When he goes to one of Lucy's sporting events, he usually brings along a book. While she is out practicing, he stays home and takes a machine apart and then puts it back together. Tom's idea of a fun afternoon is a trip to the library to read about the latest developments in science and technology. There is one thing that Tom and Lucy definitely do share. They are proud of each other. Tom thinks that Lucy's athletic talent is awesome and is going to take her far. Lucy tells everyone she knows how good Tom is with computers. These twins do have something in common!				
TOTAL				

Key: RW=Running Words   **SC**=Self-Correction   **E**=Errors

© Macmillan/McGraw-Hill

Running Record

Level __40__

Name _____ Date _____

Text __Lucy and Tom_____

Retelling Rubric

☐ **4** Accurate information, told in sequence, very detailed.

☐ **3** Accurate information, adequate detail and description.

☐ **2** Limited information, few if any details.

☐ **1** Incorrect information, little or no understanding.

Graphic Organizer: _____

Comprehension Check

1. How are Lucy and Tom different? How are they the same?

Student Response: _____

2. What do you think will happen to the twins when they grow up?

Student Response: _____

Reading Level

Error Rate $1 : \dfrac{(RW)}{(E)}$ ____ *

*Use the ratio and refer to the Conversion Table on page 7 to get a **reading accuracy percentage.**

Reading Accuracy Percentage: _____ %

Self-Correction Rate $1 : \dfrac{(E) + (SC)}{(SC)}$

Observed Reading Behaviors

- moves left to right on one line of text   ☐
- demonstrates control of one to one matching   ☐
- rereads to confirm and search for meaning   ☐
- uses intonation and expression   ☐
- uses phrasing   ☐
- uses picture cues to confirm context and visual cues   ☐

At points of difficulty, the student will _____

_____

© Macmillan/McGraw-Hill

Running Record

Running Record

Level: 40

Name: _____   Age: _____   RW: 219

Text: Earthquake! _____

Reading Accuracy Percentage: _____

Circle Reading Level: Independent   Instructional   Frustrational   SC Rate: _____

	E	SC	MSV(E)	MSV(SC)
This is a passage about earthquakes.				
Early in the morning of January, in 1994, disaster struck the city of Los Angeles. An earthquake shook the land. Bridges collapsed, buildings fell, and streets crumbled to dust. Thousands of people were left homeless. Three major highways were closed. It was one of the worse natural disasters in the history of the United States.				
The Los Angeles area has many fault lines, large cracks in Earth's crust at or below the surface. During an earthquake, blocks of crust move past each other at these lines. Sometimes the ground moves back and forth during an earthquake. At other times it moves up and down.				
104 words				
What makes the damage of an earthquake so severe? Strong tremors, or shaking movements, can cause ground to give away. Land breaks apart, landslides occur, buildings fall. Fires start when gas or electrical wiring is damaged. Things get worse when firefighters are unable to reach damaged areas to put fires out.				
In 1994 California already had many building codes to protect structures during earthquakes. After the earthquake engineers who design bridges and buildings went right to work. They were surprised to learn that many buildings and bridges had not held up as well as they expected them to. New and stronger building codes were written and enforced. The lessons they learned will help save lives.				
TOTAL				

© Macmillan/McGraw-Hill

Key: RW=Running Words   **SC**=Self-Correction   **E**=Errors

Running Record

Level <u>40</u>

Name _____ Date _____

Text <u>Earthquake!</u>

_____

Retelling Rubric

☐ **4** Accurate information, told in sequence, very detailed.

☐ **3** Accurate information, adequate detail and description.

☐ **2** Limited information, few if any details.

☐ **I** Incorrect information, little or no understanding.

Graphic Organizer: _____

Comprehension Check

I. What happens to the earth during an earthquake?

Student Response: _____

2. Why do earthquakes cause so much damage?

Student Response: _____

Reading Level

Error Rate $1 : \dfrac{(RW)}{(E)}$ *

*Use the ratio and refer to the Conversion Table on page 7 to get a **reading accuracy percentage.**

Reading Accuracy Percentage: _____ %

Self-Correction Rate $1 : \dfrac{(E) + (SC)}{(SC)}$

Observed Reading Behaviors

- moves left to right on one line of text   ☐
- demonstrates control of one to one matching   ☐
- rereads to confirm and search for meaning   ☐
- uses intonation and expression   ☐
- uses phrasing   ☐
- uses picture cues to confirm context and visual cues   ☐

At points of difficulty, the student will _____

_____

© Macmillan/McGraw-Hill

Running Record

Level: __50__

Name: _____   Age: _____   RW: __281__

Text: __Island of Purple Fruit__   Reading Accuracy Percentage: _____

Circle Reading Level: **Independent**   Instructional   Frustrational   SC Rate: _____

	E	SC	MSV(E)	MSV(SC)
This is a story about a desert island.				
Long ago a ship was exploring the South Seas, hoping to discover treasure. When a terrible storm wrecked the ship, Horace was the only survivor. He washed ashore on a desert island, and for the first few days, Horace remained where he had landed on the beach. All Horace could think about was being rescued. He was always looking out at the sea, hoping to catch a glimpse of a ship sailing over the horizon.				
After three days, though, Horace was so hungry that he decided he had to leave the beach and hunt for food. Horace searched the island from end to end but all he could find was a strange purple fruit that grew at the top of very tall trees. But Horace was worried about spending too much time away from the beach, so he quickly headed back to the shore. For the next few days, Horace sat and stared out at the sea, but he was growing hungrier and hungrier. **164 words**				
Finally, Horace decided that he had to climb one of the trees with the purple fruit. So he scaled one of the very tall trees and picked as much fruit as he could. When Horace took a bite of the fruit, it tasted sweet and delicious. It was the best fruit he had ever eaten.				
After he ate, Horace immediately fell asleep and dreamed of a large ship approaching the island. Then Horace heard voices and felt someone shaking him. It was not a dream, and Horace's rescue ship was real. The sailors helped him gather as much of the purple fruit as they could carry. Horace looked forward to going home and sharing his sweet treasure.				
TOTAL				

Key: RW=Running Words   **SC**=Self-Correction   **E**=Errors

© Macmillan/McGraw-Hill

Running Record

Level __50__

Name _____   Date _____

Text __Island of Purple Fruit__

_____

Retelling Rubric

☐ **4** Accurate information, told in sequence, very detailed.

☐ **3** Accurate information, adequate detail and description.

☐ **2** Limited information, few if any details.

☐ **1** Incorrect information, little or no understanding.

Graphic Organizer: _____

_____

Comprehension Check

1. What happened after Horace ate the purple fruit?

Student Response: _____

2. Why was Horace afraid at first to climb the tree and get the purple fruit?

Student Response: _____

_____

Reading Level

Error Rate $1: \dfrac{(RW)}{(E)}$ *

*Use the ratio and refer to the Conversion Table on page 7 to get a **reading accuracy percentage.**

Reading Accuracy Percentage: _____ %

Self-Correction Rate $1: \dfrac{(E) + (SC)}{(SC)}$

_____

Observed Reading Behaviors

- moves left to right on one line of text   ☐
- demonstrates control of one to one matching   ☐
- rereads to confirm and search for meaning   ☐
- uses intonation and expression   ☐
- uses phrasing   ☐
- uses picture cues to confirm context and visual cues ☐

At points of difficulty, the student will _____

© Macmillan/McGraw-Hill

Running Record

Running Record

Level: __50__

Name: _____   Age: _____   RW: __170__

Text: __Christopher Columbus_____   Reading Accuracy Percentage: _____

Circle Reading Level: **Independent**   **Instructional**   **Frustrational**   SC Rate: _____

		E	SC	MSV(E)	MSV(SC)
This is a time line about a famous explorer.					
1451 Christopher Columbus is born in Genoa, Italy.					
1465 Columbus becomes a sailor and takes his first voyage. He also studies navigation and mapmaking.					
1481 Columbus believes he can find a quicker route to the Far East if he sails west across the Atlantic Ocean, but he needs money to fund his expedition.					
1492 Queen Isabella and King Ferdinand of Spain agree to pay for the trip. On August 3rd, Columbus sets sail with three ships. On October 12th, they land on a small island. Columbus names it San Salvador. He also lands on what is today the Dominican Republic and calls it Hispaniola. **104 words**					
1493 In October, Columbus embarks on his second expedition. He establishes a colony on Hispaniola.					
1498 Columbus makes a third voyage to the New World, this time reaching the coast of South America.					
1502 On his last trip to the New World, Columbus sails along the coast of Central America. He is shipwrecked on the island of Jamaica for many months.					
1506 Columbus dies in Spain.					
	TOTAL				

Key: RW=Running Words   **SC**=Self-Correction   **E**=Errors

© Macmillan/McGraw-Hill

Running Record

Level 50

Name _____ Date _____

Text _Christopher Columbus_

Retelling Rubric

☐ **4** Accurate information, told in sequence, very detailed.

☐ **3** Accurate information, adequate detail and description.

☐ **2** Limited information, few if any details.

☐ **1** Incorrect information, little or no understanding.

Graphic Organizer: _____

Comprehension Check

1. Why did Columbus sail west?

Student Response: _____

2. What did Columbus need to do before his expedition?

Student Response: _____

Reading Level

Error Rate $1: \dfrac{(RW)}{(E)}$ _____ *

*Use the ratio and refer to the Conversion Table on page 7 to get a **reading accuracy percentage.**

Reading Accuracy Percentage: _____ %

Self-Correction Rate $1: \dfrac{(E) + (SC)}{(SC)}$ _____

Observed Reading Behaviors

- moves left to right on one line of text ☐
- demonstrates control of one to one matching ☐
- rereads to confirm and search for meaning ☐
- uses intonation and expression ☐
- uses phrasing ☐
- uses picture cues to confirm context and visual cues ☐

At points of difficulty, the student will _____

© Macmillan/McGraw-Hill

Running Record

Level: 60

Name: _____   Age: _____   RW: 264

Text: Ping and the Falcon _____   Reading Accuracy Percentage: _____

Circle Reading Level: **Independent**   Instructional   Frustrational   SC Rate: _____

	E	SC	MSV(E)	MSV(SC)
This is a story about a friendship between a boy and a falcon.				
In Ancient China there lived a peasant boy named Ping. Thirteen-year-old Ping was responsible for taking care of his father's goats. Ping spent every day in the fields tending to the goats. Ping found the work challenging but he was also lonely and longed for a friend.				
One sweltering summer day, as Ping was watching the goats, a beautiful falcon descended from the sky. With its wings stretched wide, the falcon circled over the boy, each time coming lower and lower. Ping waved to the falcon, and the falcon swooped down and landed on a boulder near the boy.				
After that day, the falcon visited Ping often and the boy and the falcon became friends. Ping named the great bird Chunwin. **121 words**				
Chunwin was an amazing bird because he could do tricks without any training. He just listened to Ping and did exactly what the boy said.				
Later that year, Ping heard that China was under attack by an invading army. China needed to protect its land against its enemies, so the army sent messenger pigeons into the villages to search for people willing to become soldiers. But the pigeons were stopped by the enemy's hawks.				
Ping wanted to help his country, so he told Chunwin to find the enemy's hawks and lead them away. Chunwin did as he was told. Chunwin led the hawks into the mountains and deep into a cave, where they all disappeared. Ping heard about the mysterious disappearance of the hawks. Ping never saw Chunwin again, but told everyone about the falcon's bravery and what the great bird had done.				
TOTAL				

Key: RW=Running Words   **SC**=Self-Correction   **E**=Errors

© Macmillan/McGraw-Hill

Name _____ Date _____

Text __Ping and the Falcon__ _____

Retelling Rubric

☐ **4** Accurate information, told in sequence, very detailed.

☐ **3** Accurate information, adequate detail and description.

☐ **2** Limited information, few if any details.

☐ **I** Incorrect information, little or no understanding.

Graphic Organizer: _____

Comprehension Check

1. In what way was Ping a hero in this story?

Student Response: _____

2. How did Chunwin show his loyalty to Ping?

Student Response: _____

Reading Level

Error Rate I: $\dfrac{(RW)}{(E)}$ _____ *

*Use the ratio and refer to the Conversion Table on page 7 to get a **reading accuracy percentage.**

Reading Accuracy Percentage: _____ %

Self-Correction Rate I: $\dfrac{(E) + (SC)}{(SC)}$

Observed Reading Behaviors

- moves left to right on one line of text ☐
- demonstrates control of one to one matching ☐
- rereads to confirm and search for meaning ☐
- uses intonation and expression ☐
- uses phrasing ☐
- uses picture cues to confirm context and visual cues ☐

At points of difficulty, the student will _____

_____

© Macmillan/McGraw-Hill

Running Record

Name: _____

Level: 60

Age: _____   RW: 176

Text: Madrid _____

Reading Accuracy Percentage: _____

Circle Reading Level: **Independent**   Instructional   Frustrational

SC Rate: _____

	E	SC	MSV(E)	MSV(SC)
This is a passage about Madrid, Spain.				

Location
Spain is located in the southwest corner of Europe, across the Atlantic Ocean from the United States. Madrid is Spain's capital, and is in the center of the country. The city is a connecting point to all parts of Spain. The city's two towers are called the Gateway to Europe.

Artistic Center
For years Madrid's outdoor restaurants have been a meeting place for students, artists, and writers. Madrid is an important cultural center. It has many museums, gardens, and theaters. The Prado, the largest art museum in the world, is located here. **93 words**

Madrid in Numbers
Population: 3 million
Land area: 236 square miles (about the size of Oregon)
Temperature: 42 degrees (in January) and 75 degrees (in July)

Major Products
Olives, grapes, beets, and fish. Madrid has the world's second-largest fish market.

Major Industries
Textiles, tourism, shipbuilding, and pottery making

Did You Know?
• Madrid is Europe's highest city at 2,100 feet.

• At midnight on New Year's Eve, people eat 12 grapes to the beat of the clock. This is supposed to bring them good luck.

| | TOTAL | | | |

© Macmillan/McGraw-Hill

Key: RW=Running Words   **SC**=Self-Correction   **E**=Errors

Running Record

Level __60__

Name _____   Date _____

Text _Madrid_ _____

Retelling Rubric

☐ **4** Accurate information, told in sequence, very detailed.

☐ **3** Accurate information, adequate detail and description.

☐ **2** Limited information, few if any details.

☐ **I** Incorrect information, little or no understanding.

Graphic Organizer: _____

Comprehension Check

1. What are two facts you learned about Madrid?

Student Response: _____

2. Why do you think the towers are called the Gateway to Europe?

Student Response: _____

Reading Level

Error Rate I: $\dfrac{(RW)}{(E)}$ _____ *

*Use the ratio and refer to the Conversion Table on page 7 to get a **reading accuracy percentage.**

Reading Accuracy Percentage: _____ %

Self-Correction Rate I: $\dfrac{(E) + (SC)}{(SC)}$

Observed Reading Behaviors

• moves left to right on one line of text   ☐

• demonstrates control of one to one matching   ☐

• rereads to confirm and search for meaning   ☐

• uses intonation and expression   ☐

• uses phrasing   ☐

• uses picture cues to confirm context and visual cues   ☐

At points of difficulty, the student will _____

© Macmillan/McGraw-Hill

Running Record

Level: __70__

Name: _____   Age: _____   RW: __217__

Text: __The Minotaur__   Reading Accuracy Percentage: _____

Circle Reading Level: **Independent**   Instructional   Frustrational   SC Rate: _____

	E	SC	MSV(E)	MSV(SC)
*This is a tale about an ancient creature.**				
The Minotaur, a ferocious creature that was half bull and half man, was kept in a labyrinth under the palace of King Minos. Every year seven young people from Athens were sacrificed to the Minotaur.				
One year brave Theseus volunteered to be one of the Minotaur's victims. Theseus had slain many monsters before and he was determined to kill the Minotaur.				
Ariadne, the daughter of Minos, devised a plan to help Theseus escape. At the entrance to the labyrinth, Ariadne tied the end of a ball of thread to the doorway and then gave the ball of thread to Theseus. **100 words**				
"What is that for?" asked Theseus.				
"Even if you defeat the monster, you will be wandering in the maze," said Ariadne. "The ball of thread will help you find your way back. Unwind the thread as you go, then you will be able to retrace your steps."				
Theseus could hear the Minotaur roaring the moment he stepped into the maze. Suddenly, the Minotaur was upon him. It was a difficult fight but Theseus managed to defeat the Minotaur. Then he carefully wound up the ball of thread that guided him back through the maze.				
Ariadne was waiting for him by the doorway.				
"You will be in danger for helping me," Theseus said to her. "Come with me!"				
* **Note:** Pronounce names for student before the student begins reading.				
Pronunciation Key:				
ˈMĭ-nə-tor ˈMī-nəs A-rē-ˈad-nē ˈThē-sē-əs				
TOTAL				

Key: RW=Running Words   **SC**=Self-Correction   **E**=Errors

© Macmillan/McGraw-Hill

Running Record

Level __70__

Name _____ Date _____

Text __The Minotaur__ _____

_____

Retelling Rubric

☐ **4** Accurate information, told in sequence, very detailed.

☐ **3** Accurate information, adequate detail and description.

☐ **2** Limited information, few if any details.

☐ **1** Incorrect information, little or no understanding.

Graphic Organizer: _____

Comprehension Check

1. Why did Ariadne give Theseus the ball of thread?

Student Response: _____

2. Why might Ariadne be in danger at the end of the story?

Student Response: _____

Reading Level

Error Rate $1: \dfrac{(RW)}{(E)}$ _____ *

*Use the ratio and refer to the Conversion Table on page 7 to get a **reading accuracy percentage.**

Reading Accuracy Percentage: _____ %

Self-Correction Rate $1: \dfrac{(E) + (SC)}{(SC)}$

Observed Reading Behaviors

• moves left to right on one line of text   ☐

• demonstrates control of one to one matching   ☐

• rereads to confirm and search for meaning   ☐

• uses intonation and expression   ☐

• uses phrasing   ☐

• uses picture cues to confirm context and visual cues   ☐

At points of difficulty, the student will _____

_____

© Macmillan/McGraw-Hill

Running Record

Level: <u>70</u>

Name: _____ Age: _____ RW: <u>220</u>

Text: <u>Independence Day</u>

Reading Accuracy Percentage: _____

Circle Reading Level: Independent   Instructional   Frustrational   SC Rate: _____

	E	SC	MSV(E)	MSV(SC)
This passage explains the meaning of Independence Day.				
In the seventeenth century, Britain had thirteen colonies in North America. Britain ruled the colonies and the American colonies grew and prospered.				
The relationship between Britain and the colonists began to change after the French and Indian War. The war broke out because France claimed land in North America that Britain wanted. Britain won the war.				
However, the war was expensive and Britain thought that the American colonists should help pay for it. So in 1765 the British passed the Stamp Act, which was a tax on many goods. In 1773, the British started to tax tea and then enacted other laws that the colonists thought were unfair. These events led to the start of the American Revolution in 1775. **120 words**				
In June of 1776, members of the Continental Congress met in Philadelphia. They decided it was time to officially declare America's independence.				
Thomas Jefferson was asked to write the declaration. In it, Jefferson described the rights that every man was entitled to, including "life, liberty, and the pursuit of happiness." He listed all of the colonists' grievances with Britain. Finally, he declared that the colonies were free and independent states.				
On July 4, 1776, the Declaration of Independence was approved by Congress.				
The war with Britain didn't end until 1781, but every July 4, the United States celebrates Independence Day.				
TOTAL				

© Macmillan/McGraw-Hill

Key: RW=Running Words   **SC**=Self-Correction   **E**=Errors

Running Record

Name _____ Date _____

Text __Independence Day_____

Retelling Rubric

☐ **4** Accurate information, told in sequence, very detailed.

☐ **3** Accurate information, adequate detail and description.

☐ **2** Limited information, few if any details.

☐ **1** Incorrect information, little or no understanding.

Graphic Organizer: _____

Comprehension Check

1. What were some of the events that led up to the American Revolution?

Student Response: _____

2. Why is the Declaration of Independence an important document in American History?

Student Response: _____

Reading Level

Error Rate $1: \dfrac{(RW)}{(E)}$ _____ *

*Use the ratio and refer to the Conversion Table on page 7 to get a **reading accuracy percentage.**

Reading Accuracy Percentage: _____ %

Self-Correction Rate $1: \dfrac{(E) + (SC)}{(SC)}$

Observed Reading Behaviors

- moves left to right on one line of text   ☐

- demonstrates control of one-to-one matching   ☐

- rereads to confirm and search for meaning   ☐

- uses intonation and expression   ☐

- uses phrasing   ☐

- uses picture cues to confirm context and visual cues   ☐

At points of difficulty, the student will _____

© Macmillan/McGraw-Hill

Running Record

Level: __80__

Name: _____   Age: _____   RW: __286__

Text: __Danny's Challenge_____   Reading Accuracy Percentage: _____

Circle Reading Level: Independent   Instructional   Frustrational   SC Rate: _____

	E	SC	MSV(E)	MSV(SC)
This is a story about a boy overcoming his challenges.				
The man at the reception desk looked doubtful when Danny wanted to sign up to climb and rappel the gym's rock wall. But Dad was insistent as he looked the man firmly in the eye. "My son wishes to try this sport," he said. The man shrugged his shoulders and said, "Okay. Sign here."				
Danny had one leg shorter than the other as a result of an accident when he was younger. Danny didn't walk very evenly, but the muscles in his legs were extremely strong. He desperately wanted to try climbing the rock wall and rappelling down. It was important that he find a sport that he could participate in. He wanted to be like everyone else. **118 words**				
First, Danny had to take a class in proper procedures for climbing and rappelling. He practiced wearing the harness and working the ropes. He was so excited he could hardly wait!				
Finally his chance arrived, and Danny could feel everyone's eyes on him as the ropes and harness were fastened around him. When the harness was on tight, he felt himself being lifted up and for a moment he too wondered whether he could do this.				
It was fantastic! Way up high, supported by strong ropes, traveling down in great leaps and bounds, Danny felt as free as a bird. He wished the wall were a hundred times as high, and the experience a hundred times as long. But all too soon he reached the bottom and helpful hands were loosening his harness. He set off toward his dad, unable to stop smiling or conceal his feeling of personal success.				
"Incredible" he shouted as his dad, grinning, came within hearing. "Astonishing! When can I do it again, Dad?"				
TOTAL				

© Macmillan/McGraw-Hill

Key: RW=Running Words   **SC**=Self-Correction   **E**=Errors

Running Record

Level _80_

Name _____ Date _____

Text _ Danny's Challenge _____

_____

Retelling Rubric

☐ **4** Accurate information, told in sequence, very detailed.

☐ **3** Accurate information, adequate detail and description.

☐ **2** Limited information, few if any details.

☐ **I** Incorrect information, little or no understanding.

Graphic Organizer: _____

Comprehension Check

1. Why did Danny's father insist that his son sign up?

Student Response: _____

2. Why do you think it was important for Danny to do this?

Student Response: _____

Reading Level

Error Rate $1 : \dfrac{(RW)}{(E)}$ *

*Use the ratio and refer to the Conversion Table on page 7 to get a **reading accuracy percentage.**

Reading Accuracy Percentage: _____ %

Self-Correction Rate $1 : \dfrac{(E) + (SC)}{(SC)}$

Observed Reading Behaviors

- moves left to right on one line of text ☐
- demonstrates control of one to one matching ☐
- rereads to confirm and search for meaning ☐
- uses intonation and expression ☐
- uses phrasing ☐
- uses picture cues to confirm context and visual cues ☐

At points of difficulty, the student will _____

_____

© Macmillan/McGraw-Hill

Running Record

Level: __80__

Name: _____   Age: _____   RW: __244__

Text: __Tectonic Plates_____   Reading Accuracy Percentage: _____

Circle Reading Level: Independent   Instructional   Frustrational   SC Rate: _____

	E	SC	MSV(E)	MSV(SC)
This passage explains what tectonic plates are.				
Earth's crust is broken up into large sections called tectonic plates, which float on molten rock inside the earth. The plates fit together like the pieces in a puzzle but they are constantly moving.				
Tectonic plates move in many different ways. Sometimes two plates pull apart, causing rifts and valleys, while other plates crash into each other, forming mountains. Some plates slide past each other. The places where the edges of the plates meet, or where there are cracks in the earth's surface, are called faults.				
Many of earth's features were formed by the movement of the tectonic plates. The Himalaya Mountains were created when the India Plate crashed into the Asia Plate. The Mid-Atlantic Ridge was formed by two plates pulling apart. Molten rock from inside the earth seeped out, forming the submerged mountain range. **136 words**				
Most earthquakes and volcanoes happen along the plate boundaries. Earthquakes happen most frequently in places where two plates are sliding past each other. California has experienced many earthquakes because it is on the boundary of the Pacific Plate, which is moving northwest, and the North American plate, which is moving in a southerly direction.				
Volcanoes often form in places where oceanic and continental plates converge, or meet. For example, there are many active volcanoes around the edges of the Pacific Plate, in an area that is called the Ring of Fire. Volcanoes form when magma, or molten rock, from deep inside the earth erupts through the earth's crust.				
TOTAL				

© Macmillan/McGraw-Hill

Key: RW=Running Words **SC**=Self-Correction **E**=Errors

Running Record

Name _____ Date _____

Text _Tectonic Plates_ _____

_____

Retelling Rubric

☐ **4** Accurate information, told in sequence, very detailed.

☐ **3** Accurate information, adequate detail and description.

☐ **2** Limited information, few if any details.

☐ **1** Incorrect information, little or no understanding.

Graphic Organizer: _____

Comprehension Check

1. Why has California experienced earthquakes?

Student Response: _____

2. Why do you think the area around the Pacific Plate is called the Ring of Fire?

Student Response: _____

Reading Level

Error Rate $1: \dfrac{(RW)}{(E)}$ _____ *

*Use the ratio and refer to the Conversion Table on page 7 to get a **reading accuracy percentage.**

Reading Accuracy Percentage: _____ %

Self-Correction Rate $1: \dfrac{(E) + (SC)}{(SC)}$ _____

Observed Reading Behaviors

- moves left to right on one line of text   ☐
- demonstrates control of one to one matching   ☐
- rereads to confirm and search for meaning   ☐
- uses intonation and expression   ☐
- uses phrasing   ☐
- uses picture cues to confirm context and visual cues   ☐

At points of difficulty, the student will _____

_____

© Macmillan/McGraw-Hill

Comprehension: Retell

Fill in the Retelling Chart.

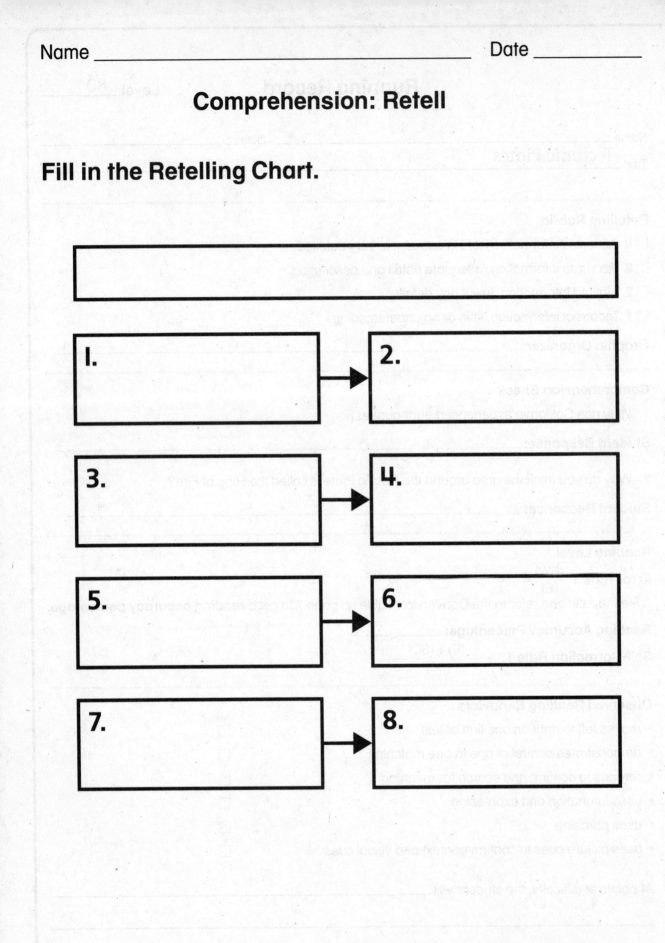

© Macmillan/McGraw-Hill

Name _____ Date _____

Comprehension: Beginning, Middle, and End

Fill in the Beginning, Middle, and End Chart.

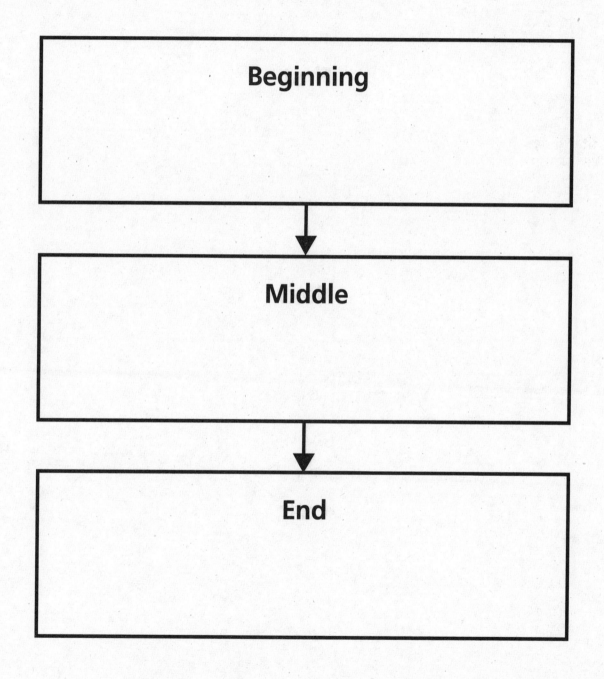

© Macmillan/McGraw-Hill

Name _____ Date _____

Comprehension: Sequence

Fill in the Sequence Chart.

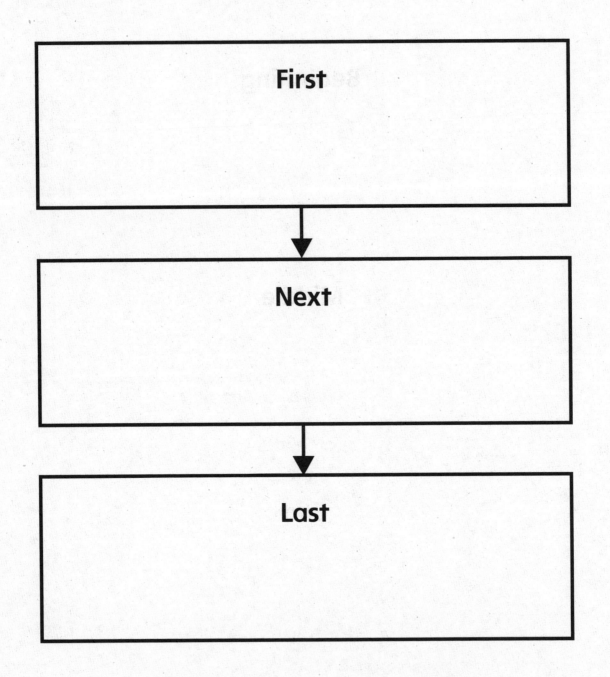

First

Next

Last

© Macmillan/McGraw-Hill

Comprehension: Summarize

Fill in the Summary Chart.

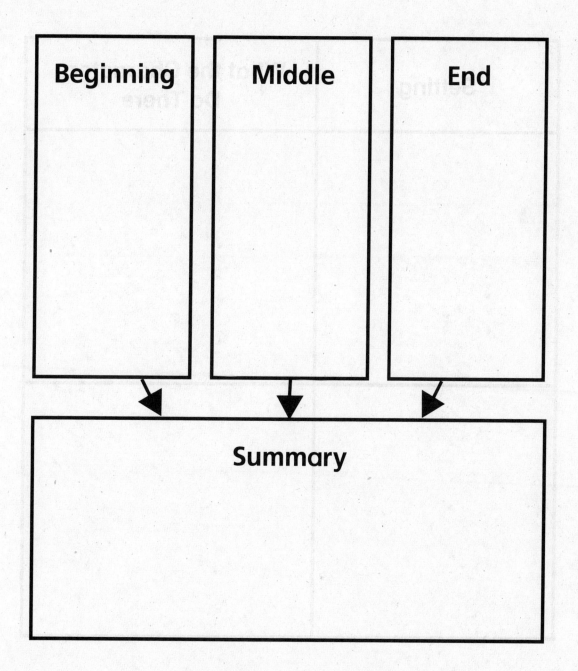

© Macmillan/McGraw-Hill

Name _____ Date _____

Comprehension: Character and Setting

Fill in the Setting Chart.

Setting	What the Characters Do There

© Macmillan/McGraw-Hill

Comprehension: Character, Setting, Plot

Fill in the Story Map.

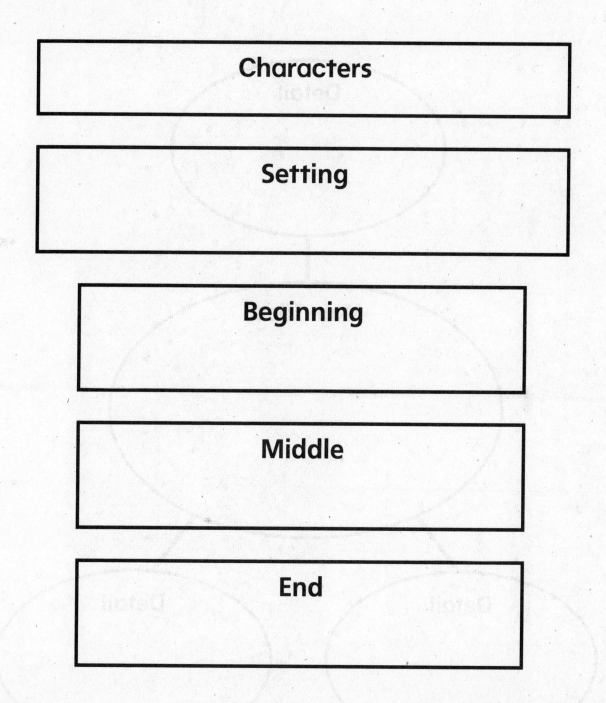

Characters

Setting

Beginning

Middle

End

© Macmillan/McGraw-Hill

Name _____ Date _____

Comprehension: Main Idea and Details

Fill in the Main Idea and Details Web.

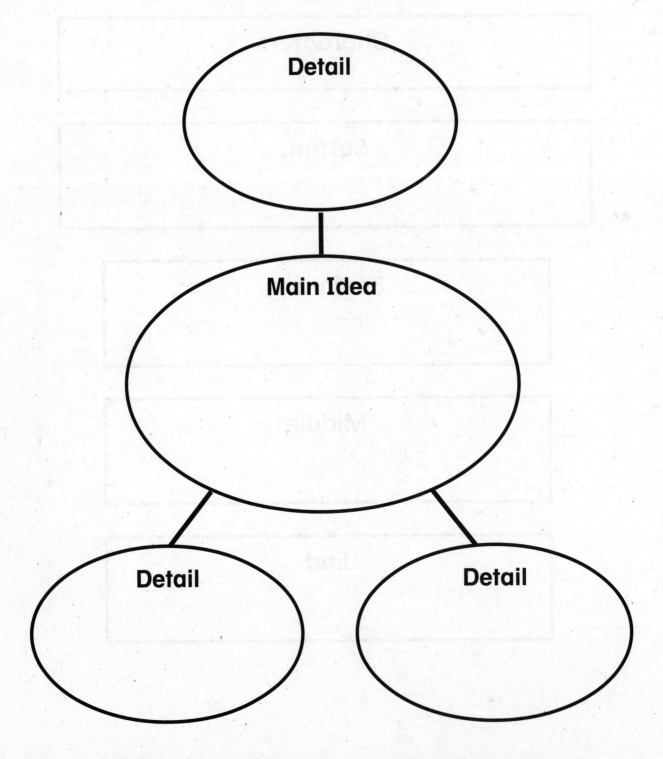

Detail

Main Idea

Detail

Detail

© Macmillan/McGraw-Hill

Comprehension: Summarize Chart

Fill in the Summary Chart.

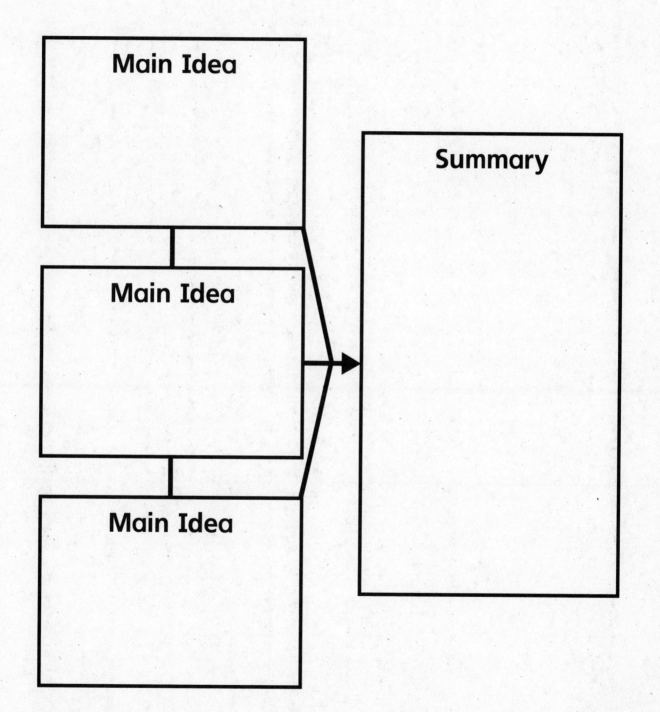

© Macmillan/McGraw-Hill

Teacher Notes

© Macmillan/McGraw-Hill